HAUNTED TEXAS

Famous Phantoms, Sinister Sites,
and Lingering Legends

Second Edition

Scott Williams
Revised by Donna Ingham

LONE
STAR
BOOKS

Guilford, Connecticut
Helena, Montana

LONE STAR BOOKS

An imprint of Globe Pequot

Distributed by NATIONAL BOOK NETWORK

British Library Cataloguing in Publication Information Available

Library of Congress Cataloging-in-Publication Data Available

ISBN 978-1-4930-2689-0 (paperback)
ISBN 978-1-4930-2690-6 (e-book)

∞™ The paper used in this publication meets the minimum requirements of American National Standard for Information Sciences—Permanence of Paper for Printed Library Materials, ANSI/NISO Z39.48-1992.

Printed in the United States of America

Some of the places described in this book are on private property. Always obtain permission in advance to visit these sites. The prices, rates, and hours listed in this guidebook were confirmed at press time. We recommend, however, that you call establishments to obtain current information before traveling.

To my children, Avery and Grace,
for keeping me motivated

TEXAS

CONTENTS

Introduction vii

Gulf Coast 1
Houston **2**
Galveston **28**
Beaumont **39**
Gulf Coast Day Trips and Getaway Weekends **45**

South Texas **48**
San Antonio **49**
Corpus Christi **73**
Victoria **84**
South Texas Day Trips and Getaway Weekends **91**

Rio Grande Valley **96**
Brownsville **97**
Laredo **105**
McAllen **112**
Rio Grande Valley Day Trips and Getaway Weekends **118**

Central Texas **121**
Austin **122**
New Braunfels **145**
Central Texas Day Trips and Getaway Weekends **155**

CONTENTS

North Texas 158
Dallas   **159**
Denton   **179**
Fort Worth   **192**
North Texas Day Trips and Getaway Weekends   **205**

West Texas   **212**
Abilene   **213**
El Paso   **228**
Lubbock   **245**
West Texas Day Trips and Getaway Weekends   **252**

Suggested Reading and Websites   **258**

Spooktacular Places to Spend Halloween   **260**

Special Indexes   **265**
Most Macabre Museums   **265**
Twitchiest Tours   **265**
Eeriest Eats   **266**
Scariest Stays   **266**

About the Authors   **268**

INTRODUCTION

Ghost hunting is becoming an increasingly popular hobby. And for some, it's even a profession. Televisions shows, books, and websites abound with ghost stories. There's something about the idea of encountering something from the world of the dead that appeals to people.

Not everyone believes in ghosts. But you don't have to actually believe in ghosts to want to add a twist to your travels around Texas or spice up your vacations.

And who wouldn't be curious about a remote-controlled car in Austin, for instance, that not only operated without a battery but also greeted guests at a downtown photography studio as if it were the owner's dog? And how do you explain the presence of so many haunted hotels in San Antonio, hotels that just happen to have been built on the site of a former cemetery?

Trying to solve these mysteries and—just as important—trying to encounter a ghost in person are what ghost hunting is all about. People who explore cemeteries late at night or descend into dark basements where some unexplained presence has been felt are driven by their desire to make sense of the unexplainable and perhaps catch a glimpse of the hereafter.

Ghosts come in all shapes and sizes. My research into Texas ghosts has turned up adult ghosts of both genders as well as the ghosts of numerous children. Those ghosts whose identities are known almost always died in some tragic accident or as the result of an illness that claimed them well before their time. Ghosts seem to prefer old houses, historic buildings, downtown districts, and cemeteries. Ghosts are not limited to the human species, however. My research has uncovered the ghost of a woman in San Antonio who has been spotted petting a phantom cat, and drivers in the Rio Grande Valley have reported seeing ghost cows by the side of the road.

Now some might say that such claims are "udderly" ridiculous. But are they? Just because you've never seen a ghost doesn't mean they don't exist. Ghost-hunting groups are popping up all over the country. They meet to tell ghost stories, investigate haunted sites, and share their knowledge of ghosts and ghost-hunting equipment. Some ghost hunters are full-fledged believers in spirits, others go on ghost hunts as a lark. Some are skeptics who go ghost hunting to prove that spooky doings can be explained by natural causes.

Although you can find numerous books filled with ghost stories at the bookstore or your local library, you'll not find many guides to haunted sites. And you definitely won't find a book quite like this one. I decided to write this book after seeing books on haunted destinations that, while interesting, were lacking in the kind of information travelers need to plan a trip around ghost-hunting excursions.

In this book you'll find haunted hotels, bed-and-breakfasts, restaurants, cemeteries, tourist attractions, and other sites scattered throughout Texas. Texas is a big state with a large population and a history wrought with conflict and struggle. People have been killed by hurricanes, wars, epidemics, and all sorts of other situations. It makes sense, then, for Texas to have so many ghost stories and haunted sites.

Listings for accommodations, attractions, or restaurants include paranormal activity, historical information (when available), and information travelers need if they want to stay at a haunted hotel or eat at a haunted restaurant. You'll also find information on sites that are *not* haunted. They've been included to make it easy to find a hotel near a haunted attraction (assuming there are no haunted hotels nearby) or a place to eat in a "normal" restaurant (assuming there are no haunted restaurants nearby) or a "normal" place to visit while taking a break from ghost-hunting activities. There are suggestions for day trips and getaway weekends to haunted sites located outside the cities covered within each region. Also included throughout the book, usually listed in the Attractions section for each city, are listings for places that are specifically open during October for Halloween and offer various sorts of scary good times.

Read on for information on when and where to find ghosts and for equipment you might want to bring on your search.

HOW TO FIND GHOSTS

As previously mentioned, ghosts seem to prefer to haunt certain types of places, although a ghost can haunt anything—or *anyone*—if it chooses. After all, who's going to stop it? The International Ghost Hunters Society claims ghosts are everywhere, and the American Ghost Society claims the most common places to find them are private homes, cemeteries, theaters, churches, schools, colleges, hotels, battlefields, crime scenes, and hospitals. You'll find all those sites inside the pages of this book.

The International Ghost Hunters Society suggests you plan your investigation near the new or full moon. The best opportunities occur two or three days before one of these moons and last until two or three days after. According to the society, this is because the lunar cycle generates the strongest geomagnetic earth fields, and since ghosts are electromagnetic in nature and part of the electromagnetic spectrum, they use geomagnetic fields to appear.

The society says another good time for ghost hunting is when a storm is approaching, although the group doesn't explain why. The staff at www.hollowhill.com, a website for ghost hunters, says ghost encounters can occur at any time, but the most active period seems to be after 8:30 p.m. and before sunrise. The theory is that there is less solar interference after the sun goes down. They've also heard reports of greater activity at the end of the year and at midnight.

The International Ghost Hunters Society says the best time to photograph ghosts is at dusk or later. A dark background is necessary to act as a backdrop for capturing ghosts on film. Contrary to what you might think, the best way to capture a ghost on film, according to the society, is by using a flash.

A good ghost hunter always comes prepared. You can spend thousands of dollars on exotic equipment, or you can choose to keep it simple. The basics include a digital camera, digital tape recorder, electromagnetic field detector, pen and paper, compass, watch or stopwatch, flour or talcum powder, and thread. Here is some additional information on each of these items:

Camera: A digital camera with at least five megapixels of resolution is recommended—the higher the resolution, the better. A camcorder and tripod are also recommended as are large-capacity memory cards.

Audio recorder: A good digital voice recorder should be used at all times. Electronic voice phenomena that are not heard during the investigation have been heard on recordings after the ghost hunt is complete.

Electromagnetic field detector: These gadgets pick up electronic fields over various frequencies. Disruptions in electronic fields can indicate the presence of a ghost. Numerous power apps that offer EMF detector functionality are available for smartphones.

Compass: Not only will a compass help keep you from getting lost, but it can also detect electromagnetic forces. Use a traditional magnetic type of compass rather than an electronic one. Traditional compasses respond to magnetic and electrical stimuli, including those that are unusual.

Watch or stopwatch: It doesn't matter what kind as long as it works and you can read it whenever you need to.

Flour or talcum powder: Use either one of these substances for capturing footprints or handprints. Sprinkle it on the ground where the investigation is taking place. It's a good idea to record the footprints of all ghost hunters so their footprints won't be mistaken for those of the ghosts.

Those who are *really* into ghost hunting might want to purchase more sophisticated equipment, such as air ion counters, headset communications, infrared thermal scanners, motion detectors, night vision equipment, night vision video cameras, and thermal imaging scopes.

You'll still have fun even if you don't have all that fancy equipment. It's also a good idea to read up on ghost hunting before you head out. Some recommended sources include:

- Ghost Hunting 101; http://ghosthunting101.com
- *The Ghost Hunter's Guidebook* by Troy A. Taylor, Whitechapel Press, 2007
- Hollow Hill; http://encounterghosts.com/hollow-hill-articles-are-here-now/
- *How To Be a Ghost Hunter* by Richard Southall, Llewellyn Worldwide, 2007

Haunted Texas is written with a dose of humor (I hope) and in a storytelling tone. So gather round, listen up, and, most importantly, watch your back. But the main thing is to have fun, be creative in the sites you select to visit, and enjoy your travels. Who knows, you may return with tales to tell and pictures to show that are out of this world.

GULF COAST

Houston

America's fourth-largest city is home to over 2 million people, and another 6.3 million live in the metropolitan area. Houston also has a fair number of ghosts, although they apparently don't like to haunt the city's hotels. The places listed in the Houston Accommodations section were chosen for their comfort and convenience to other haunted locales, such as the downtown courthouse—supposedly haunted by a U.S. district judge.

The downtown area seems to be popular among the spirits, perhaps because of the older buildings that can still be found there. Nearby Old Town Spring—on the northern edge of Houston—claims to be the ghost capital of Texas (although San Antonio has also claimed the title).

Old Town Spring is a turn-of-the-twentieth-century shopping village with more than 150 shops. It's located near the original rail yards and was built in the early 1900s by the Great Northern Railroad. Victorian-style shops such as Doll Hospital (doll repair, costuming collectibles), Just for the Birds (gifts for bird lovers), and The Wild Goose Chase (linens, lighting, folk art, and furniture) lend a nostalgic air to the town.

Houston is filled with great restaurants, shopping districts, and attractions. The area is also packed with ghost-hunting groups that can help visitors and residents learn more about the city and its ghostly inhabitants.

HOUSTON ACCOMMODATIONS

CLUB QUARTERS HOUSTON

720 Fannin Street
Houston 77002
(713) 224-6400
https://clubquartershotels.com/houston

All Club Quarters properties in major U.S. cities are private hotels located in prime downtown locations. The Club Quarters Houston is no exception. It's housed in a restored landmark building with the old-fashioned elegance that was the hallmark of early twentieth-century architecture.

Club Quarters Houston is located near Bayou Place, a trendy entertainment district with restaurants and nightclubs. It's situated near light rail, free trolleys, and the city's air-conditioned underground pedestrian tunnel system, which comes in handy on hot summer days. The theater district, convention center, and sports arena are nearby.

Although there have been no reported ghost sightings, this hotel has been around long enough to have a few ghosts roaming the halls. It's also close to the museum district attractions and the haunted federal courthouse and library (see Attractions In and Around Houston).

Hotel amenities include twenty-four-hour room service and guest service desk, a restaurant and bar, a fitness room, free high-speed wireless Internet service throughout the hotel, free use of a computer and printer, and free newspapers, magazines, and games. Room amenities include a cordless phone, tea and coffeemaker, and a desk and work area.

Bailey's Light

The highway between Angleton and West Columbia in Brazoria County isn't a place you'll want to be late at night. You might feel safe driving 70 miles an hour in your locked car, thinking that no one can reach you inside your metal cocoon, but metal and breakneck speeds can't deter a ghost if it really wants to get to you. That's why you're better off avoiding this stretch of road late at night, especially when you're all by yourself. Ghosts seem to prefer visiting people who are alone, whether to provide companionship or simply to increase their chances of scaring someone.

The ghost that haunts this area along the Texas Gulf Coast is believed to be that of James Briton Bailey, whose name was given to this flat area just south of Houston. Bailey's Prairie is haunted by what locals refer to as "Bailey's Light."

This bouncing, white ball of light floats 4 to 6 feet off the ground and has been known to chase cars.

Bailey, who went by the nickname of "Brit," was one of Stephen F. Austin's original colonists. He had a checkered history filled with charges of forgery and "antisocial behavior" before moving to Texas, and he continued his antisocial ways after arriving in the Lone Star State. Bailey liked to cause problems for Austin whenever possible and engaged in fistfights on a regular basis.

In his will, Bailey requested that he be buried standing up, with a rifle and a jug of whiskey by his side. Supposedly the slaves who dug Bailey's grave stole the jug of whiskey, and to this day Bailey haunts the area in search of his stolen jug. The light is the lantern he carries in his night wanderings in search of liquid spirits.

Bailey must have been a fast fellow—or perhaps ghosts move at a faster-than-normal pace—because when you drive this stretch of road late at night, you might find yourself being chased down the highway by a presence traveling at speeds no human could possibly attain.

No one knows why Bailey would chase a car. Maybe he thinks the driver has a bottle of whiskey, or it could be that Bailey is simply engaging in the cantankerous behavior for which he was known. Whatever the reason, it's not a good idea to stop your car along this stretch of highway unless you're prepared for a face-to-face meeting with this ornery spirit.

COMFORT INN DOWNTOWN
5820 Katy Freeway
Houston 77007
(713) 869-9211
www.comfortinn.com

This economically priced hotel is a bit of a misnomer. It's not exactly downtown, but it's close enough that the drive won't inconvenience you much. It's located close to I-10, also known as the Katy Freeway. The downtown area is 4 miles away, and The Galleria (see Attractions In and Around Houston) is a mere 2-mile jaunt.

The Comfort Inn isn't fancy. It does, however, have the basic amenities as well as a free continental breakfast, work desk with dataports, and an outdoor pool. Plus, it's close to all the downtown hauntings, such as the downtown library building, where the ghost of a former janitor can be heard playing the violin at night, and not far from I-45, which will take you north to Old Town Spring.

DOUBLETREE HOTEL DOWNTOWN HOUSTON
400 Dallas Street
Houston 77002
(713) 759-0202
www.doubletreehotel.com

This upscale hotel in the heart of downtown Houston is blocks from the Toyota Center, Minute Maid Park, the theater district, Bayou Place, and major corporations. Public spaces feature Wi-Fi for those who want wireless Internet. Complimentary downtown shuttle service and a concierge are available.

Doubletree features oversize guest rooms and floor-to-ceiling windows that offer a panoramic view of the city's downtown. There's high-speed Internet access in each room, as well as a full business center in the lobby. Rooms come with a work desk, coffeemaker, iron and ironing board, two telephones with dataports, and Web TV.

You'll find a complimentary beverage area, gift shop, lounge, fitness center, newsstand, tour desk, and shoe-shine stand inside the Doubletree. Room service is available, or you can eat at Trofi Restaurant, which describes its menu as "continental with a Mediterranean and Latin flair." It's open for breakfast, lunch, and dinner.

Doubletree is near the downtown haunts and a short (if the traffic is good) drive up I-45 to Old Town Spring.

HOLIDAY INN EXPRESS HOTEL AND SUITES
24888 I-45 North
The Woodlands 77386
(281) 681-8088
www.ihg.com

The Holiday Inn Express, located 3.3 miles from Old Town Spring, has 119 rooms and 22 suites. Amenities include free breakfast bar, voice mail, dataports, high-speed Internet access, and a business center with fax and copy machine. Same day valet service, in-room coffeemaker, hair dryer, iron and ironing board, cable TV with HBO, and a free newspaper are also available. The hotel features an outdoor pool, spa, and sauna.

ATTRACTIONS IN AND AROUND HOUSTON

BATTLESHIP *TEXAS*

3527 Battleground Road
La Porte 77571
(281) 479-2431
http://tpwd.texas.gov/state-parks/battleship-texas

The battleship *Texas* is located in the 1,200-acre San Jacinto Battleground State Historical Site in La Porte, just a few minutes east of downtown Houston. The park is home to the battleship and the San Jacinto Monument.

The monument is dedicated to those who fought for Texas independence at the Battle of San Jacinto and other places. The 570-foot-tall shaft is topped by a 34-foot star symbolizing the Lone Star Republic. It's listed as the tallest stone column memorial structure in the world and is 15 feet taller than the Washington Monument in Washington, D.C.

The *Texas,* moored in the Buffalo Bayou and along the Houston Ship Channel, is the only surviving vessel to have taken part in both world wars. It was the first battleship in the U.S. Navy equipped with antiaircraft guns and commercial radar.

The ship is haunted by a sailor named Red. Appropriately named for the color of his hair, Red appears on deck dressed in an all-white sailor's uniform. He has been seen standing near a ladder and smiling. A caretaker in the nearby trophy room claims to have once entered a space/time warp that sent her to a cemetery in Normandy. Lone Star Spirits (www.lsspi .org), an intrepid group of paranormal investigators, checked out the ship in 1998. The team reported one recorded electromagnetic field spike and came back with a photograph of an unusual streak of light.

BOB CASEY FEDERAL COURTHOUSE
515 Rusk Street
Houston 77002
(713) 250-5500

Let's hope you never have to stand trial in this downtown courthouse. It is said that the tenth floor is haunted by the ghost of the late U.S. district judge Woodrow Seals, who died following complications from open-heart surgery in October 1990.

The barrister's former chambers are said to be colder than the rest of the floor, and if you stop, close your eyes, and sniff the air, you're likely to catch a faint whiff of cigar smoke from one of the judge's stogies. Janitors and security guards often report being touched and hearing doorknobs rattling when no one is around. Others report hearing phantom voices late at night.

CHILDREN'S MUSEUM OF HOUSTON
1500 Binz Avenue
Houston 77004
(713) 522-1138
www.cmhouston.org

MSN.com has rated this as the best children's museum in the country. Located in the city's museum district near downtown, the Children's Museum of Houston hosts more than 700,000 visitors a year. It offers fourteen galleries of hands-on exhibits and innovative outreach programs.

The fun is designed for children of all ages. The Tot Spot is the place to bring your newborn, toddler, or two-year-old. A bubble machine, mirrors, and knobs, switches, and doorbells provide stimulation and experimentation for the youngest of children. Other hands-on exhibits include a TV studio, grocery store, and the Cyber Playhouse, where kids can use computers to play age-appropriate games.

CIVIL WAR MUSEUM
200 Noble Street, #6
Old Town Spring 77373
(281) 528-9911

This museum devoted to the War between the States is located in the shopping district's "Thyme Square" and is frequented not only by tourists but by the dead as well. The museum is home to the Eleventh Texas Cavalry and displays numerous Civil War artifacts. Along with its displays, the museum is also known for its reenactments of Civil War battles.

Ghosts apparently enjoy taking part in these events. Lone Star Spirits, the paranormal investigations group (see the Battleship *Texas* entry above), photographed a reenactment and later discovered a glowing orb on the film. This was no chance photograph: A psychic had directed the photographer to a certain spot after detecting the spirit of what she described as a disfigured Civil War soldier standing in the square.

DOERING COURT AND *OLD TOWN SPRING SOUVENIR*
211 Gentry Street
Old Town Spring 77373
(281) 288-4777

Some ghosts like to scare people and make them run for cover, while others simply just want to have a good time. The ghost that haunts Doering Court and the office of the newspaper *Old Town Spring Souvenir,* located in the middle of Old Town Spring, falls into the latter category. Doering Court is the spot where a man named Henry C. Doering and his wife, Ella Klein, built a home and barn in the early 1900s.

The playmate of their youngest daughter, Marilyn, is said to be the ghost behind this haunted site. Marilyn and her friend, twelve-year-old Sarah, along with a few other young girls, enjoyed playing games in the barn. One day, Sarah fell from the hayloft and broke her leg. Complications led to blood poisoning, and a few months later she died.

Locals say Sarah's spirit returns to the spot where she used to have so much fun. They also say she's waiting for her friends to join her for another game of hide-and-seek. Some people believe the girl's friends *have* returned to the barn, which is now home to the local newspaper. People who have visited the site have reported hearing children laughing and someone calling Sarah by name.

Publisher Dundy Woods and his staff have reported hearing "playful" sounds and someone scampering across the roof. The publisher also says there are times when it feels as though someone is watching him work late at night. He reports feeling cold air for no apparent reason, and sometimes when he opens the office in the morning, things on his desk have been moved.

Drop by for a newspaper. Who knows? Maybe Sarah will invite you to play as well.

THE GALLERIA
5085 Westheimer Road, Suite 4850
Houston 77056
(713) 622-0663
www.simon.com/mall/the-galleria

Got money? That should be the slogan of this upscale mall, an international shopping destination that attracts more than 30 million visitors a year. Here you'll find 375 stores, thirty restaurants, two hotels, three office towers, and a full-size ice rink made famous by Olympic champion Tara Lipinski, who trained here before winning a gold medal in ice skating at the 1998 Olympics in Nagano, Japan.

The Galleria is home to designers such as Louis Vuitton, Cartier, Chanel, and Ralph Lauren, among others. Stores include Neiman Marcus, Saks Fifth Avenue, Nordstrom, and Macy's. Bring sneakers. You'll need comfortable shoes if you plan to traverse the 2.4 million square feet inside this monster mall.

GRIFFIN MEMORIAL HOUSE/TOMBALL MUSEUM CENTER
510 North Pine Street
Tomball 77375
(281) 255-2148
www.tomballmuseum.net

The Tomball Museum Center comprises ten historical buildings, including a doctor's office, a farmhouse, a church, a gazebo, and two houses. One of the houses—the Griffin Memorial House, built before 1860—is haunted.

The ghost of a woman lives in the attic of this house and has been seen in the parlor. One of the secretaries who worked at the center saw the apparition so many times that she stopped going there alone, although the ghost never did anything threatening. The figure would sit in a rocking chair in the parlor, rocking back and forth.

Some say the ghost is the twenty-one-year-old daughter of the Faris family, who once lived in the residence. To this day, the young woman's cause of death remains a mystery.

HOUSTON MUSEUM OF NATURAL SCIENCE
One Hermann Circle Drive
Houston 77030
(713) 639-4629
www.hmns.org

This is the flagship of the city's museum district. It features the Wortham IMAX Theatre, Burke Baker Planetarium, and Cockrell Butterfly Center, as well as permanent and traveling exhibits.

The butterfly center is a replicated rain forest that everyone should visit at least once. The three-story glass conservatory is packed with vibrant, tropical plants and hundreds of live, exotic butterflies. Step inside this warm, humid enclave and you'll see between fifty and sixty different species of the world's largest and most beautiful butterflies. They flutter through the air, land on flowers, and occasionally alight on lucky visitors' hands.

Butterflies are raised on special butterfly farms in tropical Asia and North, Central, and South America. They're shipped to the center in chrysalis form.

HOUSTON ZOO
1513 North MacGregor Way
Houston 77030
(713) 533-6500
www.houstonzoo.org

The Houston Zoo is located in Hermann Park, adjacent to the museum district. It sits on fifty-five acres and houses over 6,000 animals representing more than 500 species. The zoo features a tropical bird house, children's zoo, and aquarium, along with reptiles and all sorts of animals from around the world.

The children's zoo covers the six ecosystems of Texas: the city, Gulf Coast, desert, forest, prairie, and farm. Pop-up domes allow guests to get inside a prairie dog habitat. Kids can visit a realistic bat cave or stroll on a boardwalk through a Texas forest. In the Discovery Center, children can enjoy hands-on activities.

JULIA IDESON BUILDING
500 McKinney Street
Houston 77002
(713) 247-1661
www.hpl.lib.tx.us/about/history.html

This Italian Renaissance–style building in downtown Houston was originally named the Carnegie Library when it opened in 1904 but was rechristened in honor of librarian Julia Ideson, who was head of the Houston Public Library system and worked in the system for forty-two years. It sits next door to the more modern main branch erected after the Julia Ideson Building became too crowded. The building houses the Texas and local history departments as well as special collections, manuscripts, and archives. It also apparently houses the ghost of a former janitor.

The old janitor, a Mr. Creamer, used to polish the library's reading tables and floors. He died of natural causes in the basement of the building in 1936. Legend has it that when he was alive, he would wait until the library had closed and the staff had all gone home. Then he would take out his violin that he brought from home and begin playing.

Librarians and others who use this building, which is open to the public, report hearing the sounds of violin music in the distance, especially on overcast days. They also report sometimes feeling uneasy, as though they are being watched.

MUSEUM OF FINE ARTS, HOUSTON
1001 Bissonnet Street
Houston 77005
(713) 639-7300
www.mfah.org

This museum's collection is estimated to be worth over $1.5 billion and includes art from antiquity to the present. Founded in 1900, the museum's treasures include African art and glass, American and European sculpture and painting, a Frederic Remington collection, and Chinese, Latin American, Texas, Native American, and Oceanic art.

Other highlights include antiquities of ancient Egypt, Greece, and Rome, Indonesian gold, Bayou Bend furniture, decorative arts, impressionist/postimpressionist paintings, and works from the Paris art movements of the late nineteenth and early twentieth centuries. Modern and contemporary art, photography, pre-Columbian art, and gold, textiles, and costumes are also featured. In January 2015 the museum unveiled plans for a huge-scale expansion that will include four new buildings to be completed by 2019.

OLD GREENHOUSE ROAD
Northwest Houston, 5 miles north of the Katy Freeway (I-10)

Old Greenhouse Road is not to be confused with Greenhouse Road. Old Greenhouse Road is a 1.5-mile stretch of pavement that connects Keith Harrow Boulevard with Greenhouse Road.

The ghost of an old woman who died in a car accident haunts this street at its one big turn. Legend has it that if you turn off your headlights and drive around the corner to the bridge at a slow speed, a mist forms over the bridge and condenses into the shape of a woman. If you're feeling brave enough, hang around long enough, and the ghost will approach your car. This ghost is said to prefer clear nights or nights just after a cool rain. Do you dare?

PREMIER CINEMA 11
1518 San Jacinto Mall
Houston 77002
(281) 421-8833
www.pccmovies.com/news

The staff at this multiplex on the east side of Houston says unexplained equipment failures and whisperings can only be attributed to ghosts. Those who have worked the late-night shift say they often get eerie feelings that somebody is watching them.

The computers at the ticket counter randomly go berserk at times, spitting out tickets when they're not supposed to. On numerous occasions, projectionists have reported hearing people talking and experiencing the sensation of having someone walk behind them. Sometimes movies start and stop by themselves, and the volume on the speakers goes up without explanation.

Finally, late at night, when all the projectors have been silenced, projectionists report hearing voices that sound like someone in the distance is trying to talk to them. All of these events could make for great movie material themselves!

SCREAMWORLD
2225 North Sam Houston Parkway West
Houston 77038
www.screamworld.com

Voted Houston's scariest haunted attraction by the *Houston Chronicle* and the popular website Houstonhaunts.com,

ScreamWorld offers five scary attractions all in one location: The Swamp, "considered the most high-tech haunted attraction in Houston"; the Edge of Darkness, a good ol' haunted house; Jake's Slaughterhouse (as if a traditional meat packing plant isn't bloody enough); Zombie Graveyard, capitalizing on the latest horror craze; and the Clown Asylum Maze, a superbly intricate maze that will have you screaming in no time.

SPACE CENTER HOUSTON
1601 NASA Parkway (formerly NASA Road 1)
Houston 77058
(281) 244-2100
www.spacecenter.org

Space Center Houston is the official visitor center for NASA's Johnson Space Center. It features several permanent exhibits, attractions, and theaters. Traveling exhibits and events created by the center's staff keep the place from becoming stale.

Permanent exhibits include a simulated rocket launch, a hands-on exhibit that demonstrates what it's like to live in space, a behind-the-scenes tram tour, and a collection of vintage space suits.

Kids will love the Martian Matrix, a four-story play area with a space theme. The Kids Space Place is packed with interactive stations and themed areas that give children a chance to explore different aspects of space exploration.

SPRING HISTORICAL MUSEUM
403 Main Street
Old Town Spring 77373
(281) 651-0055
http://oldtownspring.com/info/history/

This historic building sits at the entrance to Old Town Spring. It housed the city's courthouse for many years before being converted into a museum. The Old Town Spring Historical Society maintains the building and the artifacts, memorabilia, and photographs inside.

One of those artifacts is an early 1900s Victrola previously owned by Marie and Albert Paetzold. People who keep track of the town's history say Marie and Albert—who married despite her father's objections—loved to dance to records played on the hand-cranked contraption.

The loving couple died in the 1970s, but apparently their spirits live on. Members of the historical society have reported incidences in which the Victrola began playing all by itself, sending music wafting through the air. Society members also report hearing the sounds of music—apparently playing on the Victrola—after the museum has been locked up for the night. Casual observers have reported seeing a young couple inside the museum on moonlit nights dressed in wedding clothes and dancing in each other's arms.

WALGREEN'S
485 Sawdust Road
Spring 77380
(281) 363-9571

Can't sleep? This drugstore is not a prescription for insomnia. That's because it's haunted by the ghost of a former manager who was murdered execution-style during a robbery at the store in 1996. Although no one has actually seen him, employees say that sometimes in the evenings the old manager can be heard walking down the store aisles, playing tricks on employees. His favorite trick: sending stacks of diapers tumbling, just as he did while he was alive.

Several employees have reported creepy incidents while alone in the back room, too. Toys turn themselves on and off, and items fly from the shelves and break—even though no one is in the area. However, these bizarre activities have diminished since the perpetrators who killed the manager were convicted in 1998, no doubt calming this restless retailer.

The incidents haven't disappeared completely, though. Drop in after midnight. You won't have to buy any NoDoz to stay awake, guaranteed.

WHITEHALL HOME
Main and Keith Streets
Old Town Spring 77373
(832) 797-1888
http://springghosttour.com/index.html

This Victorian-style home on the corner of Main and Keith Streets was built in 1895 by the Mintz family. The two-story building, reportedly built for a mere $300, has gone through several incarnations over the years. None was more interesting than the residence/funeral parlor that the Klein family used it for in the 1930s.

After the Klein Funeral Home burned to the ground, the Klein family turned the downstairs front rooms of their home into a funeral parlor, and the downstairs rooms in the back became the embalming area. The home changed hands several more times before becoming the property of Raymond Hudson, who converted the entire building into his residence.

According to one account, the twenty-five-room house is home to a small colony of bats and a secret room is inhabited by two ghosts.

The ghosts are described as the "Courting Ghosts of White-hall." They are believed to be the spirits of a young couple who died in a car crash in 1933 on Riley Fussel Road, which crosses Spring Creek. The car ran off the road, plunging into a ravine and killing the car's two occupants.

Hikers found the couple the next day. They were taken to Whitehall Home, site of the Klein Funeral Home, and their wake and burial attracted a large, grieving crowd. According to ghost experts, dying so early may be one reason a person's spirit remains behind, because residents since then have reported strange noises coming from upstairs, and some swear they've seen a young couple in the large swing on the upstairs screened-in porch.

It's reported that the pair lives in the home's secret room and enjoys taking moonlit strolls. They also apparently enjoy scaring children. One story has it that they enjoyed frightening three young boys who built a tree house in a large pecan tree out back by shaking the tree and making ghostly noises. The boys abandoned it soon after. Remnants of the tree house can still be seen in the backyard.

The house is now owned by Chris and Ginger Pennell, who conduct regular walking ghost tours through Old Town Spring and host "Ghost Dinners and Investigations" at Whitehall Home.

HOUSTON AREA RESTAURANTS
La Carafe Wine Bar
813 Congress Street
Houston 77002
(713) 229-9399

Technically speaking, this isn't a restaurant, it's a bar. An old bar—more than 130 years old, in fact. Developer Nathaniel Kellum built the two-story structure in 1847. Then, in 1860, a man named John Kennedy opened a bakery here. This dark, old building is illuminated by dim lamps and candles sitting atop 3-foot-tall pillars of wax.

La Carafe is known for its wine list, which includes a rotating selection of reds and whites, such as cabernet sauvignon and pinot grigio. You can sit downstairs in the main room, upstairs in the small room, or outside with a view of Market Square. The second floor is where you're likely to encounter a ghost. Employees report hearing footsteps when no one is up there. They also say it sounds as if something heavy is being dragged across the floor.

In *A Texas Guide to Haunted Restaurants, Taverns, and Inns* (Republic of Texas Press, 2001), authors Robert Wlodarski and Anne Powell Wlodarski report that one employee claims to have seen a "strange-looking" woman standing at a second-floor window when he arrived for work one morning. He climbed the stairs to the second floor and found all of the rooms completely empty. They also tell the story of another worker who closed up one night and was about to head home. But something, or *someone*, made him turn around to look back toward the bar. It was then that he saw a muscular man standing at one of the windows inside. Some say it's the ghost of a former manager named Carl Prescott, who died (although not at La Carafe) in 1990.

Other strange events include exploding glasses and bottles, cold spots, and unusual shadows. Some report feeling as though they're being watched. One time two customers who were standing outside waiting for the bar to open claim to have seen a woman seated at a table inside simply disappear before their eyes.

PUFFABELLY'S OLD DEPOT RESTAURANT
100 Main Street
Spring 77373
(281) 350-3376

This American-style restaurant features a predictable selection of burgers, sandwiches, chicken, vegetables, and salads. Seafood consists mostly of catfish—grilled and fried—and shrimp from the Gulf of Mexico. You can't go wrong with Gulf shrimp, which has a much better taste than imported or farm-raised varieties. The restaurant's name derives from the children's song titled "Down by the Station." As you'll recall, the song goes: "Down by the station, early in the morning, see the little puffabellies all in a row." The puffabellies, black steam engines puffing white smoke, were a common sight in the early days. This railroad depot-turned-restaurant was originally located in nearby Lovelady and was disassembled and moved here.

The ghost of an unfortunate railroad yard switchman is said to haunt the building. The man was killed in the early 1900s while trying to flag down an engineer whose train was headed down the wrong tracks. As he ran toward the train, the switchman tripped on the rails and fell beneath the oncoming train. He lost his head—literally.

People in Lovelady began reporting strange sightings near the terminal not long after the accident. Many claimed to have seen a headless man waving a lantern and wandering around aimlessly—perhaps trying to locate his missing head—although no one could explain how a headless man could really "look" for anything.

After the building was moved to Spring, a nearby resident reported seeing eerie lights coming from the east side of Puffabelly's, the side nearest the railroad tracks. He had stopped at the railroad crossing, expecting a slow-moving train to come by, and sat in disbelief as the lights passed in front of him. He reported feeling a rush of cold air (it was August) and then spotted a headless man in overalls waving a lantern. The resident decided he had seen enough, took off, and reported the incident to police.

SPAGHETTI WAREHOUSE
901 Commerce Street
Houston 77002
(713) 229-9715

Spaghetti Warehouse is a chain of restaurants that number more than twenty in nine U.S. states. The first one began in 1972 in Dallas. Victor Petta Jr. created Italian favorites from scratch by combining recipes handed down through his family for generations.

The building that houses the Houston Spaghetti Warehouse is more than one hundred years old. It once served as a cotton warehouse and later as a pharmaceutical warehouse. The ghost investigations group Lone Star Spirits (see the Battleship *Texas* entry) reports that the owner of the pharmaceutical company died one night under mysterious circumstances. One story has it that he died near the elevator, while another version claims he died after falling into the elevator shaft.

A woman described as "the lady in white" has been seen wandering the second floor. People say she is the wife of the unfortunate victim, returning to look for her husband. Employees have reported seeing table arrangements changing before their eyes, witnessing dishes and cutlery flying off the racks in the kitchen, and feeling as though they're being watched from the stairs leading to the second floor.

But don't let that freak you out. Instead, try the Italian eggrolls. These are crisp pasta shells stuffed with Italian sausage, spices, spinach, and mozzarella cheese served with marinara sauce. Slurp up some minestrone, or try a bowl of wedding soup. This tasty concoction is made with chicken broth, diced chicken breast, spinach, noodles, and meatballs.

Have you ever had fifteen-layer lasagna? Now you can. It's handmade daily with lasagna noodles, meat sauce, and a blend of cheeses. Order spaghetti and choose from twelve sauces or a combination of two, then top it with your choice of meatballs, sautéed mushrooms, Italian sausage, melted mozzarella cheese, grilled chicken, and/or primavera vegetables.

For dessert, try the lemonberry tiramisu, made with lemons in a mixture of strawberries, blackberries, and raspberries with cream and mascarpone cheeses.

TREEBEARDS
315 Travis Street
Houston 77002
(713) 228-2622
www.treebeards.com

Make sure you visit the right Treebeards if you're looking for some supernatural action. There are four locations in Houston, but the haunted spot is at Houston's second-oldest establishment, known as the Travis Building. Built around 1870, it's located in Market Square and faces Market Square Park.

Employees report several types of ghostly activities, although they're all a bit subtle. They report hearing footsteps upstairs when no one is there and soft voices murmuring in the distance. Cold spots and the feeling that someone is watching, or following close behind, have also been reported numerous times.

Treebeards specializes in Southern cuisine. Much of it is Cajun food. Start your meal with some jalapeño cornbread and a glass of ice tea (you'll need it). Try the chicken and sausage gumbo or the grilled chicken meat loaf. It's impossible to recommend one dessert over another; choose from buttercake, yellow cake, carrot cake, and Italian cream cake.

WUNSCHE BROS. CAFE AND SALOON
103 Midway Street
Spring 77373

This American-style restaurant, housed in a former hotel/ saloon built in 1902, is currently closed, so Uncle Charlie might now be the lone resident.

The ghost of Uncle Charlie, one of three Wunsche brothers who owned the hotel and who were born to German immigrants Jane and Carl Wunsche, is said to haunt this establishment. According to legend, Charlie fell victim to unrequited love and remained a bachelor his entire life. He lived in one of the hotel's spare rooms until his death in 1915 of natural causes. A new owner took over the establishment sometime later.

A down-and-out artist is said to have lived in Uncle Charlie's room a year or so after his death. One night, he dreamed about an upset-looking old man with long white hair who wore a black hat and a matching suit and sat hunched over a table. The man then stood up and began pacing back and forth. The artist awoke at this point and, unable to sleep, decided to sketch the image in his dream.

The next day, after recounting his dream to the other guests, he showed them his sketch. They were shocked! The artist had drawn a spitting image of Uncle Charlie, despite having never met the man or seen photos of him. It must have been Uncle Charlie's ghost, they said.

Longtime residents in this area say that on still, moonlit nights, you can sometimes hear Uncle Charlie's restless spirit walking around, going from room to room. Some claim to have seen him standing at the window, and one recent owner claims to have had several encounters with the ghost. She reports encountering locked doors, seeing tables and chairs that have been turned over, and finding lost items that turn up unexpectedly.

HOUSTON ORGANIZED TOURS AND PARANORMAL GROUPS

GHOST BUSTERS OF TEXAS

www.facebook.com/texasghostbusters/

This paranormal group travels throughout the Houston area and other parts of the state to investigate haunted places. They tend to favor small towns and local spots. They also network with other paranormal groups and claim to have many members who are psychics and "sensitives" (people who can sense the presence of ghosts). The group has a collection of ghost-hunting equipment, such as electromagnetic field detectors, infrared thermal scanners, and thermal imaging scopes. You can get in touch with this group via their Facebook page. There are no dues or fees, and membership is open to anyone who's not afraid of ghosts—or at least not yet.

GHOST HUNTERS OF SOUTHEAST TEXAS (G.H.O.S.T.)

www.facebook.com/Ghost-Hunters-of-South-Texas -410695569005720/

What a great name for a ghost-hunting group! Here you can meet fellow ghost hunters, share stories, and join together for organized investigations of haunted places in the Houston area. Members often share mysterious images captured on film. You can keep track of G.H.O.S.T., post questions, and keep up-to-date on paranormal investigations conducted by the group via their Facebook page.

South Texas Paranormal Society
www.southtexasparanormalsociety.com

This society describes their organization as "a team of Paranormal Investigators that network with fellow paranormal investigators all over the United States in an effort to expand knowledge, share resources, and bring respect and unity to the paranormal field." They offer free investigations to individuals in Texas who are concerned about supernatural or other inexplicable experiences.

Lone Star Spirits Paranormal Investigations
www.lsspi.org

Founded in 1997, Lone Star Spirits uses high-tech equipment such as thermal imaging cameras, surveillance equipment, motion-triggered cameras, and handheld devices to detect atmospheric changes while investigating haunted sites. They've investigated places throughout Texas and report their findings on their website.

Pete Haviland, the group's lead investigator and president, is a certified clinical hypnotist who has helped clients remove fears, anxieties, and psychological triggers that, according to the website, have "caused either possible poltergeist activity, or hypersensitivity, due to subconscious triggering mechanisms."

Walking Ghost Tours of Old Town Spring
Doering Court
100 South Main
Spring 77373
(800) 979-3370
http://oldtownspringghosttours.com/home.html

Ninety-minute tours take visitors to the many haunted places in Old Town Spring (see Attractions In and Around Houston), a turn-of-the-century shopping village with more than 150 shops located near rail yards built in the early 1900s. Victorian-style shops lend a nostalgic air to the town and, at night, give the place an unmistakable creepy feeling. These walking tours cost $25 per person, with a minimum of four people required. Kids under age five (if you choose to bring yours) can take the tour for free. You can book your tour by checking the calendar on the website. Most tours are offered at 8:00 p.m. and 9:30 p.m. year-round.

Galveston

Galveston is the name given to both the barrier island off the coast of Texas and the city that is found there. It is about an hour's drive from Houston and a popular vacation spot for visitors who like beaches and the downtown historic district.

The Strand Historic District (or simply The Strand) is packed with Victorian-era buildings occupied by retail stores, restaurants, nightclubs, bars, and coffee shops. Other popular Galveston attractions are Moody Gardens and Schlitterbahn Galveston Island Waterpark.

French pirate Jean Lafitte used Galveston as the base for his smuggling operations in the 1800s. The island was captured by Union soldiers during the Civil War and later retaken by their Confederate counterparts.

Galveston served as the state's largest and most important city until a hurricane in 1900 known as the Great Storm hit, killing an estimated 6,000 of the city's 37,000 residents and destroying some 3,600 buildings. Following the storm, people and businesses moved inland to Houston.

Galveston is a bright, cheerful place by day. At night, especially in The Strand, things can get a bit creepy after the crowds disperse and the lights dim. Ghosts are said to roam a haunted room in a popular hotel, while the spirit of a slain police officer is said to haunt the former bank building where he was killed. Don't worry, though; Galveston's ghosts have never been known to harm anyone. At least, not yet.

GALVESTON ACCOMMODATIONS

THE HOTEL GALVEZ & SPA—A WYNDHAM GRAND HOTEL

2024 Seawall Boulevard
Galveston 77550
(409) 765-7721
www.hotelgalvez.com

The Hotel Galvez, which opened in 1911, sits right on the city's seawall overlooking the Gulf of Mexico. Once known as the "Queen of the Gulf," this early twentieth-century marvel has hosted such famous guests as U.S. president Teddy Roosevelt, billionaire Howard Hughes, and singer Frank Sinatra—as well as an infamous unknown apparition.

Visitors and staff say The Hotel Galvez has a haunted room. It's room 505. Patrons say they get so creeped out here that they sometimes cut their visits short. They also say the scent of gardenias can be detected in and near the room.

At least one guest has reported being so scared that she says she'll never stay there again. It all started one night when she was staying at the hotel with her three children. After going to bed, the speaker button on the phone suddenly turned on, and the sound of a dial tone filled the room. The guest turned on the light, turned off the speaker phone, and, once she had calmed her nerves, turned off the light.

It happened again.

"It wasn't until I actually told 'it' to stop and prayed aloud for God's help with the matter that I was finally able to turn off the lights with no hair-raising occurrences," the woman said. "The next morning I asked the front desk, and they said many people have had similar experiences and it's to be expected in an old hotel. Unless you are seeking an experience beyond our world, I would recommend you stay away from the fifth floor!"

She's obviously not cut out to be a ghost hunter.

Aside from the occasional ghost or two, a $9 million renovation has returned the eight-story hotel to its former glory. Its 226 rooms include elegant touches, such as marble bathrooms, hand-decorated walls, and Gulf views. Rooms also come with modern amenities, such as high-speed Internet access and cordless telephones.

The hotel is a free trolley ride from downtown, art galleries, museums, and the shops and restaurants of The Strand. Galvez Bar & Grill, the hotel's on-site eatery, is open for lunch and dinner. It features Gulf Coast seafood with an ocean view.

THE QUEEN ANNE BED & BREAKFAST
1915 Sealy Avenue
Galveston 77550
(409) 497-4936
www.bedbreakfasthome.com/galvestonqueenanne

This Victorian-style gem is situated a few blocks from The Strand, theaters, restaurants, the island's cruise terminal, and some beautiful beaches. Stained-glass windows, 12-foot-tall ceilings, inlaid wood floors, and period antiques characterize this home, built in 1905. And so does the "tall, thin" ghost that never bothers anyone and seems to be content simply floating around the different rooms.

On numerous occasions he has been spotted leaving one of the guest rooms, walking down the hall, and disappearing into another room. This unnamed apparition appears to be harmless and seems to enjoy technology.

Per the *Ghostly Gatherings Newsletter,* ghosts seem to be inordinately fascinated with new gadgets and gizmos. The computer in this B&B's office seems to attract the ghost's attention on a regular basis. The spirit has been spotted more than once watching closely as someone taps, taps, taps the keyboard.

Other ghostly occurrences include the sound of footsteps, a rocking chair that begins moving on its own, and a shadowy form seen moving through walls. In *A Texas Guide to Haunted Restaurants, Taverns, and Inns*, authors Robert Wlodarski and Anne Powell Wlodarski describe an incident in which a brass ring atop a candleholder suddenly shot up into the air and landed on a table. They also tell the story of an elderly man sitting outside one morning smoking a cigarette. He realized he needed a tissue and said so aloud to himself. Out of nowhere, a tissue dropped into his lap. The ghost is apparently a stickler for cleanliness: When the elderly man returned to the porch to retrieve the tissue, it had disappeared.

The B&B's six suites come with a private bath—including two with Jacuzzis—individual climate control, robes, and tourist information. A second-floor sitting room has a television, DVD player, and games. Freshly brewed coffee is available for guests who rise before breakfast, and hot tea and cookies are available throughout the day. Breakfast is served on antique china. Soft music and candlelight make greeting the day a wonderful experience. A full breakfast is served daily, including homemade breads, jams, jellies, and praline sauce.

GALVESTON ATTRACTIONS

Ashton Villa House

2328 Broadway Street
Galveston 77550
(409) 765-3402
www.galvestonhistory.org/attractions/architectural-heritage/
ashton-villa

The Ashton Villa was the first of Galveston's great mansions, setting the standard for those that followed. Built in 1859 by James Moreau Brown, a wholesale hardware merchant, railroad corporation president, and banker, the Italianate-style home was one of the most magnificent in the state at the time of its completion.

The home is filled with period antiques, family heirlooms, and original art—and multiple nineteenth-century ghosts. Visitors report seeing both male and female ghosts dressed in Edwardian clothes. They also report hearing disembodied footsteps and unidentified noises, and experience the feeling that they're not alone. Brown's daughter, Bettie, who liked to hold impromptu piano recitals, is believed to be one of these apparitions. She enjoys switching ceiling fans on and off and likes to leave otherworldly handprints on the bed covers when no one is looking. Employees continually find the bedcovers askew despite the fact that the beds are off-limits.

A caretaker once reported awaking in the middle of the night to the sound of a piano. He entered the house and followed the music to the Gold Room, where he saw a hazy image of a woman seated at the piano. The mysterious woman soon faded into nothingness. Furniture in this home has been known to move from one place to another, and sometimes clocks stop without reason.

Although the house is no longer open to the public for guided tours, it can be rented out for weddings and other special events.

1839 SAMUEL MAY WILLIAMS HOUSE
3601 Avenue P
Galveston 77550
(409) 762-3933
www.galveston.com/samuelmaywilliams/

The Williams House is a strange mix of design—and unexplainable cold spots. Part Creole plantation, part New England–style homestead, the Williams House is named after the founder of the Texas Navy (who served as secretary under Stephen F. Austin, the man credited with founding the first Anglo-American colony in Texas).

The home is listed on the National Register of Historic Places and is a Recorded Texas Historic Landmark. Samuel May Williams died on September 13, 1858, at the age of sixty-three, without a will. His four surviving children divided the property and sold the house. It remained in the second owner's hands until 1953, when the Galveston Historical Foundation purchased it. In 2007 it was sold and is now a private residence.

The Williams House is believed to be haunted by Samuel May Williams, although no one has actually seen him. His ghost manifests itself in cold spots and a "strange, uncomfortable energy," according to Lisa Farwell, author of *Haunted Texas Vacations*. She writes that numerous tourists have felt a strong presence along with cold spots outside the children's bedrooms. Another report has it that Williams can be seen strolling the third-floor balcony.

EWING HALL, UNIVERSITY OF TEXAS MEDICAL BRANCH
301 Avenue E
Galveston 77550
(409) 772-1011
www.utmb.edu

This concrete-and-sandstone building on the UTMB campus is said to contain the image of an old, bearded man who appears on the eastern side of the building. Some say it's the image of pirate Jean Lafitte, who sailed in these waters. Lafitte was described as the "gentleman pirate" who ran his operations out of New Orleans and, later, Galveston. He claimed to never have plundered American ships and was credited with helping to defeat the British at the Battle of New Orleans in 1815. Although involved in the slave trade, Lafitte is best known for robbing merchant ships and supposedly hid his treasure in Louisiana's swamps and bayous.

The face appears in shadow form. Efforts by the university to sandblast the image from the surface of the outside wall have been thwarted, with the image reappearing a short time after it's removed. The outside wall in question is composed of nine 7-by-10-foot grids. The image covers one entire grid.

The eastern side of the building faces the Gulf of Mexico. Perhaps Jean Lafitte's spirit has staked claim to a good spot for gazing out to the sea where he spent so many exciting years.

MOODY GARDENS GALVESTON ISLAND
One Hope Boulevard
Galveston 77554
(800) 582-4673
www.moodygardens.com

Moody Gardens is like an amusement park without rides, unless you count the IMAX Ridefilm Theater, which rocks and shakes viewers to make them feel as though they're inside the movie they're watching.

Moody Gardens features a ten-story Rainforest Pyramid re-creating a tropical environment. Palm Beach offers a white sand beach with a blue lagoon, where kids can swim and play. The Discovery Pyramid is home to interactive exhibits that allow visitors to enjoy learning about science.

The Aquarium Pyramid features 100,000 square feet of exhibit space. A multi-phase renovation began in August 2015 and was slated to be completed at the end of May 2017.

SCHLITTERBAHN GALVESTON ISLAND WATERPARK
2026 Lockheed Drive
Galveston 77550
(409) 770-WAVE (9283)
www.schlitterbahn.com

The people behind the Schlitterbahn water parks (there are four in Texas) started in New Braunfels in Central Texas, creating what the Travel Channel has dubbed the best water park in the nation.

The Galveston site is open year-round thanks to a heated 70,000-square-foot area with a convertible roof. This area, known as the Wasserfest, includes four tube slides, three speed slides, three kids' activity areas, a surfing area, a beach, a giant hot tub, and an artificial river.

A recent addition to the park—the Blastenhoff—includes a river with rapids, a new kids' play area, a hot tub, and a large speed tower featuring three body slides. Parking is free, and you can bring picnic baskets into the park. Glass containers and alcohol are not permitted.

GALVESTON RESTAURANTS
GAIDO'S SEAFOOD RESTAURANT
3802 Seawall Boulevard
Galveston 77550
(409) 761-5500
www.gaidos.com

Gaido's began its life as a sandwich shop in a Galveston bathhouse in 1911. S. J. Gaido, the great-grandfather of the current owners, named it after himself. Four generations of Gaidos have dedicated themselves to the family business,

transforming it into one of the most popular seafood restaurants in the state.

Its vast menu of fresh seafood, much of it caught in the
nearby Gulf of Mexico, is complemented by homemade sauces,
salad dressings, and desserts made from old family recipes. Gaido's also has an extensive wine selection that includes a La Crema
chardonnay flavored with citrus and spiced apple. The atmosphere is somewhat classy (think white tablecloths), but diners
are welcome to dress casually, and reservations are not accepted.

Recommendations include "iced" shrimp (Gulf shrimp
boiled in spices, cooled over ice, and served with cocktail
sauce), dinner salad with pecan vinaigrette, and your choice
of fish charcoal grilled with olive oil and herbs. The menu also
includes combination seafood dinners, chicken, steak, pasta,
and oysters.

Desserts you might want to try include the pecan ball
(vanilla ice cream, sugar cinnamon pecans, homemade caramel
sauce, and whipped cream) and *cassatta con cioccolato bianco*
(alternating thin layers of angel food cake and lightly whipped
sweet ricotta white chocolate cream served with Gaido's homemade raspberry sauce and fresh fruits). Bring your appetite!

MEDITERRANEAN CHEF
2402 Strand Street
Galveston 77550
(409) 765-7700
www.galveston.com/mediterraneanchef/

Greek food is the specialty of this restaurant in The Strand.
Although some Texans might be shocked to hear it, the steak
wasn't invented in Texas. Greeks apparently enjoy them,
too—at least that's the conclusion one must draw based on
the selection here.

Recommendations include fried cauliflower (deep fried and served with tahini sauce and pita bread), shrimp kebabs, moussaka (potatoes and ground beef blended with wine and spices, covered with eggplant, and topped with béchamel sauce), and baklava.

The ghost that haunts this restaurant (housed in what was once a bank) is the spirit of a police officer killed while trying to foil a robbery in 1920, according to *The Gator Press*, a local publication. On October 2, 1920, a robber followed an armored car to the bank and attempted to rob the armored-car guard when he stepped out of his vehicle.

The guard ran inside, followed by the thief, who encountered Galveston police officer Daniel Brister, who happened to be inside. The robber killed Officer Brister during the ensuing gun battle. It is Brister's ghost that is believed to haunt the place. Employees say the ghost is mischievous. He turns off freezers and plays with the lights. Perhaps the police officer is letting his more playful side show after a life spent fighting crime.

THE SPOT
3204 Seawall Boulevard
Galveston 77550
(409) 621-5237
http://thespot.islandfamous.com

Burgers, sandwiches, and seafood (mostly fried) dominate the menu at this casual diner overlooking the Gulf of Mexico. The founders built this restaurant and shopping area out of three vacant houses that were scheduled to be demolished.

They moved the houses to a vacant lot, refurbished and painted them, and converted them into a combination retail/ restaurant compound. The Spot is now owned by Dennis Byrd, an island native, who began working at the restaurant as a cashier and eventually purchased it in 2002.

The Spot offers a good selection of lunch and dinner items served indoors or on one of the largest open-air decks on the island, where you can dine or enjoy a beverage from the bar while gazing out at the Gulf of Mexico. Try the crab-stuffed jalapeños, shrimp and sausage gumbo, and a Ralph Burger (made with cheddar cheese, bacon, barbecue sauce, and pickles).

If you survive all that, finish yourself off with a piece of caramel fudge cheesecake or key lime pie for dessert.

GALVESTON ORGANIZED TOURS AND PARANORMAL GROUPS

GHOST TOURS OF GALVESTON

Twenty-fifth Street and Santa Fe Place
(281) 339-2124 or (409) 949-2027
http://ghosttoursofgalvestonisland.com

Ghost Tours of Galveston is touted as the city's "longest and mostly widely respected" historical and haunted tour. It even won a Silver Award for the Best Guided Land Tour in the galveston.com Best of Galveston 2014 Awards.

Founder Dash Beardsley, who describes himself as the "Ghost Man of Galveston," began offering ghost tours in 2000. He now offers three walking tours of The Strand and a local cemetery, as well as a bus/tram tour of Galveston Island. He mixes Galveston history with island ghost stories.

Cameras are encouraged, but video cameras and tape recorders are forbidden. The tour is recommended by the Galveston Historical Society and the Galveston Visitors Center for its accuracy and entertainment.

Check out the website for additional information and to book your tour.

Beaumont

Beaumont is a place where Texas and Louisiana culture comes together. While proud of their Texas pedigree, many people here point to their Cajun ancestors across the border to explain their affinity for boiled crawfish, red beans and rice, and jambalaya.

Located northeast of Houston, Beaumont is a city of approximately 117,500 people. Beaumont, Port Arthur, and Orange form what's called the Golden Triangle, a major industrial area on the Gulf Coast. The city is located on Texas's coastal plain 30 miles inland from the Gulf of Mexico. It's also a few miles southeast of the thick pine forests of East Texas, including the "Big Thicket," a dense section of forest that is now a national preserve.

Beaumont was named by Henry Millard for the family of his deceased wife, Mary. Millard came to Texas in 1835 and purchased land that became Beaumont. Oil was discovered at nearby Spindletop on January 10, 1901, setting off an oil boom and creating one of the nation's first major oil fields.

BEAUMONT ACCOMMODATIONS
LA QUINTA INN BEAUMONT MIDTOWN
220 I-10 North
Beaumont 77702
(409) 838-9991
www.lq.com

The 122-room La Quinta is located off I-10, 5 miles from downtown and near several tourist attractions. Guests receive a free continental breakfast in the lobby. You can save money on meals by cooking your own entrees on the guest grill near the outdoor pool.

Amenities include a safe deposit box at the front desk, photocopy machines, free parking, a business center, and a twenty-four-hour front desk. Rooms come with complimentary toiletries, free high-speed Internet access, voice mail, cable/satellite TV, tea and coffeemaker, desk, hair dryer, iron, and ironing board.

MCM ELEGANTE HOTEL
2355 I-10 South
Beaumont 77705
(409) 842-3600 or (877) 842-3606
www.mcmelegantebeaumont.com

Like most other Beaumont hotels, the MCM Elegante is located on I-10, 5 miles from the Beaumont Municipal Airport, in the central part of town. Hotel amenities include a fitness center, outdoor pool, free breakfast, room service, gift shop, and business center.

You can eat, drink, and be merry at Hemingway's Restaurant and the Tradewinds Tavern, or get a caffeine boost at the Starbucks Coffee Bar. Guest rooms come with four-poster beds, 13-inch pillow-top mattresses, leather chairs, and leather ottomans. Other amenities include ergonomic chairs, cable TV, voice mail, free HBO, high-speed Internet access, and two telephones.

An iron and ironing board, hair dryers, coffeemakers with gourmet coffee, and lotions, shampoos, and soaps from Bath & Body Works make your stay here as comfortable as home, maybe more so. The nine-story, 277-room hotel also provides guests with a car rental desk, business center, and hot tub.

BEAUMONT ATTRACTIONS
Big Thicket National Preserve
6044 FM 420
Beaumont 77705
(409) 951-6725
www.nps.gov/bith

This 97,500-acre preserve was set aside in 1974 by the federal government to protect the abundant wildlife here. It's home to eighty-five tree species, more than sixty types of shrubs, and almost a thousand different flowering plants. Ferns, orchids, and four of North America's five types of insect-eating plants are found here.

More than 180 varieties of birds live or migrate through the preserve, and 50 reptile species—including a small population of alligators—live within the protected area. Activities include hiking, bird watching, biking, camping, boating, horseback riding, hunting, kayaking, and swimming.

Bragg Road Light
Bragg Road, Saratoga (40 miles northwest of Beaumont)

Hundreds of people have witnessed a "ghostly" light that appears on this dirt road that travels north to south through this forested area. The light hovers for a while and then zooms past or, in rare instances, alights on the hood of a car.

Bragg Road is located on the west side of Saratoga, a town of 1,300, and runs north, connecting Texas Highway 105 with Highway 1293.

The road began as a path carved out by the Santa Fe Railroad in 1902. The company laid tracks so that trains could carry people, cattle, oil, and logs from this area known for pine logging and oil exploration. Loggers took all the virgin pine in the area, and the oil boom went bust, so the Santa Fe Railroad stopped train service and ripped up the tracks. The county later made a road out of it.

Tales of the ghost light began in the 1940s and grew. Some say the light is a lantern carried by the ghost of a railroad engineer decapitated by a train. The headless man is in search of something. Is it spare change? His car keys? No, he's searching for his head! Don't lose yours. A trip to this dark, desolate stretch is best shared with friends armed with searchlights and sneakers.

Some say the light is a phenomenon that occurs in areas where the spirits of Spanish conquistadors are searching for buried treasure. Others say the light is the remainder of a fire that never died out or the ghost of a man shot during a Civil War incident that became known as the Kaiser Burnout. The Kaiser Burnout is named for a Confederate captain who set fire to the forest to flush out locals who refused to serve in the military.

FOREST LAWN MEMORIAL PARK
4955 Pine Street
Beaumont 77703
(409) 892-5912

This cemetery on the northeast side of the city is home to the "Kissing Statues." The story has it that the statue of a young man and woman, used to mark the grave of two of the cemetery's long-lost lovers, comes to life at night. The two begin kissing whenever someone shines a light on them.

A website devoted to Beaumont's now-closed French High School (www.fhsbuffs.com) includes a description of one former student who decided to visit the cemetery at night.

"Beth" said she and her son drove to the cemetery at 1:30 a.m. armed with a video camera and searchlight. She said they had no trouble finding the statue.

They drove past it and saw nothing unusual. The second time around, though, they saw the statue of the woman move. They aimed their searchlight at the statue and then:

> My son and I both gasped out loud as we saw his head—not hers—turn around and look at us. I couldn't believe my eyes, so my son—being a big macho man and not afraid of anything—starts to get out of the van and, with the light, walks toward the statue. The closer he got, the weirder it looked, and then we heard a noise. I screamed and he ran back to the van to check on me. Once he got in the van, I took off.

SIGMA PHI EPSILON HOUSE AT LAMAR UNIVERSITY
4400 Martin Luther King Boulevard
Beaumont 77703
(409) 880-7011

The Texas Epsilon chapter was founded at Lamar University in 1957. The house the fraternity brothers reside in was originally built by a farmer, who considered it his dream house. Legend has it that it served as a bordello following the farmer's death. The fraternity purchased it in the late 1980s.

"SigEps" who have lived at the house claim to have seen a ghost dubbed "Chester," although that seems to be a name given to him in jest rather than the name of a real person. Fraternity brothers say Chester likes to wait until the place is almost empty before knocking on bedroom doors, opening and closing other doors, and walking up and down the stairs.

The creaking caused by an invisible presence gives guys the creeps, but they say Chester is kind and believe he protects them from harm.

BEAUMONT RESTAURANTS

KATHERINE & COMPANY

1495 Calder Avenue
Beaumont 77701
(409) 833-9919
www.katharineandcompany.com

This quaint gourmet sandwich shop began as a take-out catering business in 1997. As the business grew, it moved to the historic Mildred Building complex and began serving lunch Monday through Friday. Katherine & Company offers salads, soups, entrees, vegetables, and desserts. Low-fat and vegetarian foods make this a healthy choice. South Beach and Atkins Diet followers will find options here to prevent them from straying from their diets.

The Mildred Building is named after the daughter of oil tycoon Frank Yount. A designated historical landmark, this Mediterranean-style building is accented with sixteenth- and seventeenth-century Spanish influences, as evidenced by the building's crests and wooden beam motif. The complex includes an eighteen-unit apartment building and an adjacent business arcade connected by a fenced courtyard.

Try the mango salad made with mangos, avocado, goat cheese, bacon, and pine nuts served on a bed of greens and topped with lemon dressing. The roasted vegetables and hummus in a pita pocket and the wild rice with dried cranberries and apricots make for a good meal. For dessert, try the crème brûlée, miniature cheesecakes, and fruit tarts or one of the many varieties of homemade cookies.

GULF COAST DAY TRIPS
AND GETAWAY WEEKENDS

Your best bet for a haunted day trip or weekend getaway would be to take a drive to **Nacogdoches** (pronounced nac-a-DOH-chis). This town of 30,000 in East Texas is 140 miles northeast of Houston and 127 miles north of Beaumont.

Nacogdoches is the oldest town in Texas. Evidence of human settlement dates back 10,000 years. The Caddo Indians settled there in 700 BC, and it later became one of the first European areas of development in the region.

The town is home to **Stephen F. Austin State University,** named for the man who led the first Anglo settlement in Texas. It's here at this university of 13,000-plus students that you'll find most Nacogdoches ghosts (try saying "Nacogdoches ghosts" three times fast).

A ghost named "Chester" haunts the **W. M. Turner Auditorium.** He is not believed to be the same Chester who haunts the Sigma Phi Epsilon House at Lamar University in Beaumont (see Beaumont Attractions). This Chester is said to be one of three people: the architect who designed the auditorium, a construction worker who helped build it, or a drama student who performed there. Other less popular theories claim Chester may have been a solider in the Texas Revolution, the Civil War, or one of the battles the Caddo Indians fought at the site, although it seems unlikely that a Caddo Indian would name anyone "Chester."

The architect theory goes like this: Construction workers supposedly misread his blueprints and constructed the auditorium (part of the fine arts building) backward. The architect was so humiliated and angry over the incident that he killed himself. Talk about a bad day at the office!

The story behind the demise of the drama student is unknown. The most interesting aspect of this story has it that when the drama department planned its first performance of *Hamlet*, the student chosen to play the ghost fell ill. The director searched for someone to replace the student and chose the only other person who knew the lines. History doesn't say how the director found this person or who it was, but a cast photo taken later that night supposedly revealed only a faint glow where the person portraying the ghost had been standing.

Chester's face has been seen on the stage curtain. There is no record of a description of what Chester looks like, but he also is said to show up as a ghostly extra in plays. Odd noises and cold spots are attributed to him.

The Texas Ghost Hunters website (www.texasghosthunters .com) lists another building said to be haunted. **Griffith Hall** is the site of the ghost of a female resident assistant who jumped to her death from a third-floor window after playing with a Ouija board. No one knows what the mysterious talking board said to her. Obviously, it wasn't good news.

Her spirit is said to haunt the floor. Residents have reported seeing a girl in tattered clothes standing at the end of the hall. When they turn back to look at her a second time, she's gone. Residents also say the lights flicker in the communal shower area at the same time each night, and residents in the south wing report hearing footsteps around 2:00 a.m. Perhaps this is around the time she jumped from her window!

Need a place to stay? Try the **Holiday Inn Express Hotel & Suites** (3807 South Street, Nacogdoches 936-564-0100). The rooms are large and comfortable. An outdoor pool with rock waterfall is a nice touch. So is the fireplace in the great room off the hotel lobby. Sink into the comfortable couch, sip a hot beverage, and watch the flames. You'll be able to sleep soundly because there aren't any ghosts here—at least not yet.

Two of the better places to eat in town are right next to each other. One is **Auntie Pasta's** (211 Old Tyler Road, Nacogdoches, 936-569-2171, www.auntie-pastas.com), and the other is **Clear Springs Cafe** (also at 211 Old Tyler Road, 936-569-0489, www.clearspringsrestaurant.com). Auntie Pasta's serves traditional Italian food, including a ten-layer lasagna and handmade pizzas. Clear Springs Cafe serves country foods like chicken-fried steak and fried catfish, shrimp, and oysters. You can also get blackened catfish, grilled steaks, and Cajun gumbo.

SOUTH TEXAS

San Antonio

Remember the Alamo?

Texans do. Living Texans—and dead ones too. Anyone who knows the story of the Alamo won't be surprised to learn that it's haunted. This former Spanish mission is a shrine to one of the bloodiest battles in the fight for Texas independence. One hundred and eighty-nine Alamo defenders and 1,600 Mexican troops died during the thirteen-day siege.

Afterward, there were so many bodies—including those of pioneer legends Davy Crockett and Jim Bowie—that most didn't receive a proper burial. Instead, they were dumped into mass graves, rolled into the San Antonio River, or piled up and burned. Many say the spirits of these displaced souls wander the area, troubled by their violent and untimely deaths.

Martin Leal, a ghost hunter and owner of a popular ghost-hunting tour company in San Antonio called Haunted History of San Antonio Ghost Hunt, says the Alamo's history— and the fact that the area in front of the Alamo once served as a cemetery—explains why it and the downtown are so haunted.

"It seems like ghosts are attracted to certain things," says Leal, "like battlefields, cemeteries, and hotels." The Menger Hotel on one side of the Alamo and the Emily Morgan Hotel on the other are both said to be haunted. The Emily Morgan Hotel has even more reason to attract spirits, Leal says, because it began as a hospital.

In the past decade or so, the ghost tourism industry has practically risen from the dead in Texas. When darkness arrives, these companies take visitors on walking tours through downtown San Antonio to visit haunted sites and search for ghosts with special ghost-hunting equipment, such as electromagnetic field detectors and temperature sensors that can tell the temperature of an area 100 feet away. Customers are allowed to try out these gizmos at the end of the tour. Alamo City Paranormal Ghost, another one of Leal's companies, investigates ghosts in San Antonio and the surrounding area.

Ghosts aren't the only things San Antonio is known for. Named for the river of the same name, San Antonio is home to the beautiful Paseo del Rio, or River Walk, a collection of shops and restaurants along the river in the city's downtown. SeaWorld San Antonio, Six Flags Fiesta Texas, and authentic Mexican cuisine are popular here too.

Keep reading for more information on ghosts and other activities in San Antonio and the surrounding area. After visiting the state's self-proclaimed "Most Haunted City in Texas," you may not remember the Alamo, but you'll never forget your first encounter with a real live—or should we say "dead"—ghost.

SAN ANTONIO ACCOMMODATIONS

COURTYARD BY MARRIOTT SAN ANTONIO DOWNTOWN/ MARKET SQUARE

600 Santa Rosa South
San Antonio 78204
(210) 229-9449 or (800) 706-0253
www.marriott.com

Courtyard by Marriott is an economically priced motel for those who expect to spend most of their time ghost hunting and sightseeing rather than lounging around the room. Located in the city's downtown, Courtyard by Marriott reflects the region's Mexican influences, with white walls to reflect the sun's heat and a red-tiled roof influenced by Spanish architecture.

This 137-room, 12-suite motel is a mile from the River Walk and steps from El Mercado, a collection of colorful shops selling Mexican wares. Amenities include free parking, high-speed Internet access, an oversize work area, in-room coffee, and a hair dryer. The Bistro is an on-site casual restaurant open for breakfast and dinner, and you can stock up on snacks and beverages from the twenty-four-hour food market. You'll have to do lunch at a nearby restaurant, though. Mi Tierra (218 Produce Row, 210-225-1262), a Mexican restaurant open for breakfast, lunch, and dinner, is a short walk away. Or visit Biga on the Banks (203 South St. Mary's Street, 210-225-0722, www.biga.com), where New American cuisine is served for those looking for an upscale dining experience. Reservations are encouraged—and leave your jeans at the hotel.

If a long day of ghost hunting doesn't keep you fit, try out the exercise room or swim a few laps in the pool.

EMILY MORGAN HOTEL
705 East Houston Street
San Antonio 78205
(210) 225-5100
www.emilymorganhotel.com

This 177-room luxury hotel, named for the woman who is said to be the inspiration for "The Yellow Rose of Texas," faces the Alamo complex, allowing guests in the Plaza Suite to soak in their in-room Jacuzzi while gazing out at the cradle of Texas liberty. Light some candles. Open a bottle of wine, and, perhaps after a few glasses, you may see a ghost crossing the Alamo grounds.

Ask for the ghost hunters' discount and you'll get a variable discount (depending on the season and other factors) and a room in an area with the most ghost activity. Ask for a room on the seventh floor, and perhaps you'll receive a visit from one of the ghosts said to frequent this former hospital. Or visit the hotel's lobby late at night and search for cold spots, apparitions, and unusual noises. Other ghostly activities include slamming doors and toilet lids and moving objects. One of the elevators supposedly is plagued by a mischievous poltergeist. Although no one has ever seen him, this poltergeist has been known to make calls to the front desk from the elevator phone and push buttons to make the elevator go up and down.

Hang out in the hallways and you might be lucky enough to run into the ghost of a teenaged girl who for unknown reasons asks guests to follow her to the fourteenth floor, then turns and disappears. Those with weak hearts may want to avoid the basement, which was once used as a morgue. People have reported hearing voices in the basement and the sound of footsteps that could not be accounted for. Most people avoid this area, but they're not ghost hunters.

The hotel's namesake, the fair Emily, is said to have "distracted" Mexican general Antonio López de Santa Anna at the Battle of San Jacinto. General Santa Anna was literally caught with his pants down, enabling the Texas revolutionaries to defeat the Mexican army.

Built in 1926 at a cost of $1.5 million, this ornately sculpted stone and terra-cotta structure (check out the terra-cotta gargoyles that suffer from toothaches and other medical woes—clues to the building's past) was renovated in 2001 and now gleams.

The building's narrow footprint and imposing Gothic Revival detailing give this thirteen-story building the illusion of being much taller than it is. It's located in downtown San Antonio within walking distance of the San Antonio Convention Center, the River Walk, and Rivercenter Mall.

Amenities include saunas, whirlpool, and an exercise room, as well as a bar and restaurant serving an eclectic menu of seafood, beef, chicken, and wild game. The Executive Suite and Plaza Suite come equipped with minifridges, Jacuzzi bathtubs, and king-size beds.

MARRIOTT PLAZA
555 South Alamo Street
San Antonio 78205
(210) 229-1000 or (800) 421-1172
www.marriott.com

It's unusual for a relatively new hotel like this one to have a ghost, but it does. (For some reason, ghosts seem to favor old places with spooky architecture.)

The Marriott Plaza is a modern hotel, and the ghost story associated with this facility isn't easy to find. Even longtime San Antonio ghost hunter Martin Leal hadn't heard of this one. But the folks at ghosttraveller.com list this place as the site of a double hanging.

It seems a woman hanged herself and her luckless feline, which had obviously used up its other eight lives before its owner slipped over the edge. The woman's ghost is now said to haunt the Marriott. She wears a long white nightgown and has been spotted in the hotel's upper levels, the employee corridors, the basement, and the garden. You can tell it's her instead of an overly pasty guest because she's holding her cat and stroking its head. If she doesn't make the hairs on the back of your neck stand up, at least give the Marriott Plaza extra points for having the only known feline ghost in Texas.

The Marriott Plaza is located across the street from Hemisfair Park and Tower of the Americas. Courtyards, gardens, and fountains lend a tranquil air to this property, which is equipped with a swimming pool, whirlpool, sauna, exercise room, and outdoor playground. You can even play croquet on the hotel lawn.

The oversize rooms, most with a balcony, come with high-speed wireless Internet access, cable/satellite TV, and bathrobes. The Plaza King Deluxe overlooks a beautifully landscaped courtyard where five restored historic buildings have been converted into meeting facilities.

MENGER HOTEL
204 Alamo Plaza (at Crockett)
San Antonio 78205
(210) 223-4361 or (800) 345-9285
www.mengerhotel.com

In 1859 (only twenty-three years after the battle for the Alamo), William Menger, who ran a brewery, built the Menger Hotel to accommodate his guests—who often succumbed to deep, drunken slumber after sampling too much of his brew. Throughout the intervening years, seven additions have been made to the hotel, which now boasts some 350 rooms.

History buffs will remember that Theodore Roosevelt recruited many of his Rough Riders (a name given to the volunteer cavalry unit that served under Roosevelt in the Spanish-American War) in the Menger Hotel bar. What is less common knowledge is the story of Sallie White, a chambermaid shot by her jealous husband on March 28, 1876, and buried at the hotel's expense. Sallie is said to roam the third floor of the original wing (primarily at night), wearing a long gray skirt and bandanna. She is usually carrying towels, although she never seems to actually deliver them anywhere.

Other ghost stories are told of the Menger and the property surrounding it. The newest rooms face the Alamo, and guests have witnessed ghosts wandering the grounds from their windows overlooking Alamo Plaza.

Be sure to visit with longtime employees such as Ernesto Malacara, the Menger's director of public relations, who have compiled a litany of ghost stories sure to give you goose bumps. They'll tell you stories of bumps in the night, kitchen utensils that fly through the air, and visits from people whose presence can be felt but not seen.

Captain Richard King, founder of the 825,000-acre King Ranch in South Texas, has been spotted by many entering the King Suite via a wall in the same spot where a door to the suite once stood.

Another story tells of a guest who stepped out of his shower and walked into the bedroom to find the figure of a man dressed in a buckskin jacket and gray trousers. The apparition spoke to someone whom the man couldn't see. "Are you gonna stay or are you gonna go?" he asked three times, before disappearing into thin air.

Could this be the ghost of Davy Crockett? Legend has it that the Alamo defenders were offered the chance to leave the former mission and save their lives or stay behind to face certain death. Was this the ghost of Davy Crockett asking another Alamo defender what he planned to do?

Then there is the story of a lady who was sitting in the Menger Hotel lobby, quietly knitting. She was wearing metal-framed glasses and an old blue dress and beret with a tassel. An employee asked, "Are you comfortable? May I get you something?" The lady, speaking in an angry voice, said no and disappeared.

Along with Teddy Roosevelt, the Menger has hosted such notable citizens as Babe Ruth, Mae West, Robert E. Lee, Ulysses S. Grant, Sarah Bernhardt, and Gutzon Borglum (the creator of Mount Rushmore).

The Menger, the oldest continually operating hotel west of the Mississippi River, is located downtown, adjacent to the Alamo and the Rivercenter Mall. Its three-story Victorian lobby is worth a visit even if you aren't staying there. Polished marble floors reflect light from the hotel's nearby courtyard. A mezzanine provides an expansive view of the lobby, which is decorated with western paintings, sculptures, and antique furnishings.

Amenities at this five-story hotel include the Colonial Room Restaurant, the Menger Bar, one of downtown San Antonio's largest swimming pools, a full-service spa, a fitness room, and a Jacuzzi.

Red Roof San Antonio Downtown
1011 East Houston Street
San Antonio 78205
(210) 229-9973
www.redroofinnsanantonio.com

This low-priced motel is on the east side of I-37, which is something of a psychological barrier separating visitors from the popular downtown area. Don't let that stop you. The downtown tourist/ghost attractions are within walking distance if you don't mind a moderate hike.

This six-story inn was remodeled in 2015 and features an outdoor, unheated pool and interior corridors. Some rooms come with minifridges. All rooms come with coffeemakers, cable TV, and Wi-Fi.

Sheraton Gunter Hotel
205 East Houston Street
San Antonio 78205
(210) 227-3241 or (866) 716-8134
www.sheratongunter.com

First opened on November 20, 1909, the Sheraton Gunter Hotel recently celebrated over nine decades of continuous operation and $8 million in renovations. It also is home to what may be the most infamous haunted room in San Antonio.

According to legend, in 1965 a man checked into room 636. A few days later, after he checked out, the hotel's maid found the room soaked in blood. Witnesses claimed to have seen the man carrying a bundle, and a search of the room turned up a bullet hole in one wall. The man reportedly had been seen earlier in the company of an attractive blonde, who had previously been spotted entering and leaving the hotel with him.

In his room, police found receipts for purchases, including, to their horror, a meat grinder. A few days later, they received a tip that he had checked into another hotel. As police closed in to arrest him, the mysterious murderer committed suicide.

The ghost of the murdered woman is said to haunt the hotel.

The Gunter Hotel is named for Jon Gunter, who put together a group of investors to build it. Gunter believed a palatial structure was needed to meet the demands of the state's most progressive city.

The twelve-story Gunter Hotel is across the street from the beautifully restored Majestic Theatre. Amenities include a restaurant, pasta bar, fitness center, whirlpool, outdoor heated pool, and game room/arcade. This 322-room hotel is not far from the Alamo, the River Walk, the San Antonio Convention Center, El Mercado, and the Spanish Governor's Palace.

THE ST. ANTHONY—A WYNDHAM HISTORIC HOTEL
300 East Travis Street
San Antonio 78205
(210) 227-4392
www.thestanthonyhotel.com

The St. Anthony looks like it should be haunted. One visitor remarked that the hallways reminded him of the hotel in the Stephen King horror story *The Shining*. Built in 1909, the restored St. Anthony features beautiful carpets, bronze statues, and art from around the world. The dated appearance of this hotel, although elegant by day, takes on a more foreboding character once night falls. It's easy to imagine bats flying from its upper-floor windows and ghosts seated in the French Empire antiques that decorate the lobby.

Ghost experts say the St. Anthony is haunted by several spirits. The most famous may be the old woman whose black shoes were visible under the door to a stall in the public bathroom. Open the door and what do you see? Nothing. So many uninvited guests came to see the phenomenon that the St. Anthony finally replaced the partial door with one that goes all the way to the floor.

Guests now have to settle for spotting other ghosts, such as the one of a man who is usually seen standing in a doorway to one of the rooms near the elevator. However, whenever he is spotted, he then turns quickly and walks through the door to one of the guest rooms—without bothering to open it.

Other ghosts rumored to haunt the St. Anthony, according to ghosttraveller.com, are Anita, a former employee, newlyweds who sound as though they're still enjoying their honeymoon, and a sad woman who haunts the Anacacho ballroom. Ghostly guests, dressed in early twentieth-century clothes, also have been spotted in the Anacacho.

The sounds of children's laughter from the hotel's roof are said to come from ghosts, and don't be surprised if you step onto an elevator and find a transparent woman dressed in red accompanied by a man in a top hat and tails.

The St. Anthony combines the elegance and grandeur of a historic hotel with the amenities modern travelers demand. Rooms come with pillow-top mattresses, lighted headboards, high-speed Internet access, and many other amenities.

SAN ANTONIO ATTRACTIONS
THE ALAMO
300 Alamo Plaza
San Antonio 78205
(210) 225-1391
www.thealamo.org

The first ghosts reported at the Alamo appeared after Mexican general Antonio López de Santa Anna ordered the mission destroyed. He gave the job to General Juan José Andrade, whose men reported six diablos guarding the fort. These devils, they said, were screaming at them and waving flaming sabers.

James L. Choron writes in a story published on www .texasescapes.com that other frightening events reported at the Alamo include screams, the sound of explosions, and faint notes of "El Deguello," the Spanish call of "no quarter" that Santa Anna is said to have ordered to be played before the final assault.

Some have reported seeing a Mexican general wandering the grounds, saddened by the carnage that took place, Choron writes, and a man and a child have been spotted on the roof. Guests at nearby hotels claim to have seen ghosts traipsing across the grounds in the early morning hours when everyone is supposed to be sleeping. On one side of the Alamo Defenders Monument is a depiction of a ghost dubbed the "Spirit of Sublime Heroic Sacrifice."

Whether or not you believe in ghosts, there's no doubt that the Alamo was witness to fearsome fighting. Originally a mission known as Misión San Antonio de Valero, construction began on the Alamo in 1724.

In December 1835, Ben Milam led Texian and Tejano volunteers against Mexican troops quartered in the city, forcing them to flee. The victors occupied the by-then-fortified Alamo, leading to the arrival of General Santa Anna and his army of several thousand.

The defenders held out for thirteen days until the predawn morning of March 6, 1836, when Mexican soldiers attacked the garrison several times. The Mexicans scaled the walls and overwhelmed the compound.

Today, the Alamo is a shrine to these fallen heroes maintained by the Daughters of the Republic of Texas. The chapel—the famous facade recognized around the world—and the Long Barracks are all that remain of the original fort.

FEARESTA (FORMERLY NIGHTMARE ON GRAYSON)
3363 East Commerce
San Antonio 78220
www.fearesta.com

With as many ghosts as San Antonio has, it's no surprise that Halloween here is celebrated with haunted houses and costume parties. Once known as the longest-running haunted house in San Antonio, Nightmare on Grayson was closed to make way for redevelopment of the area in late 2012. However, the props and scares have since been moved into a larger venue and dubbed Fearesta. This fun-filled, spirited festival embraces the scary while providing enough family- and kid-friendly entertainment to be enjoyable for all ages. The festival is held Friday and Saturday nights from late September through Halloween and features various delights—food and drink, freak shows, face painters, and a newly added Ouija board museum.

McNay Art Museum
6000 North New Braunfels Avenue
San Antonio 78209
(210) 824-5368
www.mcnayart.org

McNay Art Museum, housed in the late Marion Koogler McNay's Spanish Colonial Revival home, focuses primarily on nineteenth- and twentieth-century European and American art. Cézanne, Picasso, Gauguin, Matisse, O'Keeffe, and Cassatt are featured in the museum, which sits on twenty-three acres adorned with fountains, broad lawns, and a Japanese-inspired garden and fishpond.

McNay's ghost is said to haunt the west wing. Security personnel report having heard a woman humming in that area, and the guards say visitors have reported seeing the transparent figure of a woman in the first-floor women's restroom.

SeaWorld San Antonio
10500 SeaWorld Drive
San Antonio 78251
(800) 700-7786
https://seaworldparks.com/en/seaworld-sanantonio

One of three SeaWorld adventure parks in the nation, SeaWorld San Antonio is the world's largest marine life adventure park, with more than twenty-five shows, educational experiences, rides, and attractions. It's home to its own Shamu, the famous killer whale featured at each SeaWorld, and her companion whales, which perform in the 4,500-seat Shamu Stadium.

The 250-acre park is filled with shows, exhibits, and attractions. It includes a water park where you can don a bathing suit and cool off in pools, slides, and water rides. You'll also find a roller coaster and several other nonwater rides.

SeaWorld is open daily during the summer and weekends during spring and fall. Check the website for the latest prices and online discounts. Dates and hours vary.

SIX FLAGS FIESTA TEXAS

17000 I-H 10 West
San Antonio 78257
(210) 697-5050
www.sixflags.com/parks/fiestatexas

This theme park in the western part of San Antonio features shows and rides placed in Hispanic, German, western, and rock 'n' roll settings. The 200-acre park, located in an old rock quarry, features 100-foot cliffs as a backdrop and offers musical entertainment at various shows throughout the day.

The Superman Krypton Coaster is the largest steel and only "floorless coaster" in the Southwest. It features 4,000 feet of twists, turns, spiral loops, and corkscrews at speeds as fast as 70 miles per hour. The Rattler, a wooden roller coaster that takes riders as high as 180 feet off the ground, is another popular ride.

October is the "spookiest" month to visit, with shows, decorations, and other frightening features designed to scare visitors in a friendly sort of way. Check the website for prices and online specials. Dates and hours vary.

SPANISH GOVERNOR'S PALACE

105 Military Plaza
San Antonio 78205
(210) 224-0601
www.sanantonio.gov/CCDO/parksplazas/governorspalace.aspx

Built in 1722 to protect the Alamo and its surrounding colony, the Spanish Governor's Palace became the seat of the Tejas

(Texas) government for the Spanish Province. It also served as the capitol building for the Tejas region until the declaration of Texas independence was signed, thus creating a new government.

The website for San Antonio Ghost Tours, a touring company that specializes in ghost tours of San Antonio (www .alamocityghosttours.com), claims the Spanish Governor's Palace sits in an area that "has seen as much death and murder per square foot as anywhere on earth."

The grounds include the "tree of sorrow," named for the forty-six convicted criminals said to have been hanged from its branches. Their faces have supposedly begun to appear in the trunk of this tree, their eyes bulging from their sockets.

A maintenance man who works at the palace claims to have heard a woman crying and other noises coming from a well where the body of a murdered woman was dumped in the 1800s. The man also claims that chairs are moved in one of the hallways in the palace at night.

Visit on the last Sunday of the month and you'll be greeted by La Compania de Cavalleria del Real Presidio de Bexar, a living-history group that wears uniforms and carries *escopetas* (shotguns) similar to those of the early Spanish soldiers. They answer questions and educate visitors about the Spanish occupation of Texas.

VICTORIA'S BLACK SWAN INN
1006 Holebrook Road
San Antonio 78218
(210) 590-2507
www.victoriasblackswaninn.net

Despite its name, this "inn" is actually a rentable event venue on thirty-five acres of lawns and gardens, filled with oak and pecan trees. Built in 1867, the building's exquisite charm is reflected in its crystal chandeliers, antiques, and gleaming hardwood floors . . . and in its ghosts. The inn can be used for all sorts of events, including "hauntingly romantic" weddings.

When proprietor Jo Ann Rivera first purchased the property, she was awakened nightly by the apparition of a man standing at the foot of her bed. Too frightened to do or say anything, she simply stared back at the man until he disappeared a few seconds later. Ever since, unexplained phenomena—including lights turning on and off, music coming from the walls, and doors locking and unlocking on their own—have been commonplace.

The inn is built on the site of the 1842 Battle of Salado, and perhaps it is the ghosts of the dead combatants, or those who lived and died in the Native American dwellings found there, that haunt the grounds.

Ghost tour leader Martin Leal has done six television shows at the inn, and on four of those occasions he heard unexplained knocking. Leal and the TV crew members experienced the unexplained draining of batteries that were supposed to last three hours and held up for only three minutes. He says a ghost hangs out in the first bedroom on the left as you enter, and thermal imaging by members of his crew detected a cold spot on a staircase where the ghost of a woman has been seen by previous visitors. Perhaps it's the ghost of Joline Woods Street, who succumbed to cancer at an early age. Her bedroom was located upstairs to the left of the stairs, and those who have seen her describe her as a beautiful woman dressed in 1920s garb.

The ghosttravelers.com website reports that paranormalists, investigating the inn for a TV program, caught an "electronic voice phenomenon" of a man saying, "Oh, shut up!" It also reports that a workman in the south part of the basement complained of the apparitions of little children taunting him and poking him with sticks.

WITTE MUSEUM
3801 Broadway
San Antonio 78209
(210) 357-1900
www.wittemuseum.org

A ghost thought to be that of Ellen Schulz Quillen, founder of the Witte Museum, apparently doesn't like the way the staff handles things these days. Employees report papers being moved and doors unlocked, and a shadowy figure has been seen moving across a room. Noises have also been heard in the museum's attic that sound like footsteps and the scraping of a chair across the floor.

The Witte is an older, comfortable museum that is particularly fun for kids. It's heavy on natural science, history, and anthropology, with sensory feedback exhibits that let visitors participate.

It also has a log cabin and large exhibit on ancient Texans—the prehistoric Indians of the lower Pecos—and a science tree house.

SAN ANTONIO RESTAURANTS
ALDO'S RISTORANTE ITALIANO
8539 Fredericksburg Road
San Antonio 78229
(210) 696-2536
www.aldossa.com

This romantic, candlelit restaurant is located in a century-old home filled with antiques, with a beautiful lounge and a small tree-covered patio where you can enjoy flowers, trees, or a starlit night.

El Muerto

The name alone is scary enough.

"El Muerto," Spanish for "the dead," is the moniker given to this legend of the South Texas brush country. The story dates back to as far as the 1850s, and witnesses have reported seeing the awful spectacle as recently as 1969. A couple traveling to San Diego, Texas, via covered wagon in 1917 reported an encounter with the ghoul.

Camped for the night, the couple sat near the fire as sleep drew near—that is, until the sound of a galloping horse chased the sleep away. The sound of an approaching horse was odd enough, especially at night, but a galloping horse in the darkness could mean only one thing: trouble.

The man grabbed his rifle as his wife moved closer to him for protection and comfort. Who could it be? And what did the rider want? The sound of the horse grew nearer, and then, out of the darkness, a gray mustang appeared— its head up, its ears thrown back in sheer terror.

A dark figure sat atop the horse. The couple squinted into the night to try to see the man's face before the awful realization sunk in: The rider had no head! The headless rider bounced up and down with the rhythm of the galloping horse. The man raised his rifle to fire and then saw something that caused him to freeze.

Strapped to the horse's back, in front of the rider, was a severed head with a sombrero firmly attached. The head bounced from side to side as the horse got closer. The man was too shocked to fire. Not that it would have mattered: The rider not only had no head, but his corpse was riddled with bullet holes and punctured by a dozen or more arrows.

The horseman rode past without slowing down.

"It is mine! It is all mine!" he shouted, then continued off into the darkness. The couple didn't sleep much that evening. After arriving in San Diego the next day, they shared their experience. Longtime residents exchanged knowing glances and then explained that they had not been the first people to encounter such a rider.

Stories like theirs had cropped up for decades, ever since Texas Rangers Creed Taylor and "Big Foot" Wallace caught a man named Vidal who had stolen cattle and horses. Livestock theft was considered a crime punishable by death in the 1800s. The Rangers, however, wanted to do more than punish the man. They wanted to make an example out of him in hopes of putting an end to the thievery.

So they cut off his head, strapped the corpse to a wild mustang, and set the horse loose. Stories of the headless horseman began to crop up not long after that, and the legend lives on long after the horse was captured and the beheaded corpse was laid to rest.

The food here is top-notch Italian. The service can be slow during busy times, but the waitstaff is always attentive and helpful. Aldo's serves up excellent minestrone, filet mignon, and a grilled portobello mushroom topped with balsamic vinegar and served with polenta.

For dessert, try a serving of tiramisu, or go wild with some cinnamon-infused Mexican chocolate mousse with bananas.

THE CHURCH BISTRO AND THEATRE AT KING WILLIAM
1150 South Alamo Street
San Antonio 78210
(210) 271-7791
www.churchbistroandtheatre.com

Built in 1912, this building housed the Alamo Methodist Church until 1968.

It's listed on the National Register of Historic Places. Located in the King William Historic District near downtown, it's surrounded by beautiful mansions and quaint cottages built by the German immigrants who helped found San Antonio.

The most frequent ghostly visitor to this restaurant/theater is Miss Margaret, who always appears in a white, Victorian-style dress with lace collar, leg-of-mutton sleeves, and full-length skirt. She almost always shows up during a stage production, leading many to believe she's the ghost of the late Miss Margaret Gething, a San Antonio resident who stepped in for an ailing actress when a touring show visited the city in the early 1900s. Miss Margaret died in 1975, a year before the lady in white began appearing at this San Antonio landmark.

Ask your waitperson to see the Polaroid photo a tourist snapped of her in 1995.

One of the most popular ghosts at this former church, previously known as the Alamo Street Restaurant and Theatre, is Eddie, the ghost of a young boy who died of polio. Eddie enjoys tearing through the house making all sorts of noise, especially in the kitchen, where he is said to playfully push employees into the walk-in refrigerator. Other ghosts include Al Martin, a man dressed in a dark suit, and an elderly man who hangs out in the belfry.

Spooky occurrences include cold spots, lights going on and off, washed and drained dishes suddenly moving back into the dishwasher, unusual noises, and doors opening and closing and locking and unlocking themselves.

The all-you-can-eat lunch buffet features fresh vegetables, pastas, and at least four different entrees each day. Dinner theater performances are held at night, and reservations are required. Tickets can be purchased for dinner and the performance or just the performance.

LA FOGATA

2427 Vance Jackson Road
San Antonio 78213
(210) 340-1337
www.lafogata.com

Mexican food, not Tex-Mex, holds sway here. La Fogata's vast menu includes an assortment of appetizers, soups and salads, quesos and quesadillas, enchilada plates, grilled specialties, a selection of signature dishes, traditional Mexican plates, sweets and pastries, and various soft and alcoholic drinks.

Try the cebollas al carbon (green onions cooked over a charcoal flame) for an appetizer, and, if you're in the mood for soup, order the caldo de pollo (soup with shredded chicken breast, Mexican rice, and avocado).

From the grill, try the tacos al carbon (grilled chicken or beef mixed with green onions, beans, Mexican rice, and pico de gallo). For a signature dish, you can't go wrong with the chile en nogado (poblano pepper stuffed with picadillo, almonds, and green olives covered with pecan sauce).

La Fogata is also known for its thirst-quenching margaritas and relaxed atmosphere. Sit outside under shade trees or the covered patio, or dine inside with white tablecloths and soft lighting.

MORTON'S, THE STEAKHOUSE
Rivercenter Mall
300 E. Crockett St.
San Antonio 78205
(210) 228-0700
www.mortons.com

This upscale dining establishment features dark wood, celebrity photos, and waiters clad in tuxedos. Morton's specializes in classic fare with generous portions of USDA prime aged beef. You'll also find fresh fish, lobster, and chicken entrees.

No need to bring your reading glasses here. Morton's brings the menu to your table via carts bearing every menu item, which the waiter then describes in great detail.

Morton's slow-roasted prime rib is served on Friday and Saturday nights. Traditional side dishes include baked potatoes, creamed spinach, and steamed broccoli with hollandaise. The desserts at Morton's are fairly standard. You'll find cheesecake, carrot cake, coconut cake, and apple pie. For something a little different, try the molten chocolate cake or the raspberry cake.

SCHILO'S DELICATESSEN
424 East Commerce Street
San Antonio 78205
(210) 223-6692
www.schilos.com

A storefront deli atmosphere prevails here, where generations of San Antonians have come for German-style delicatessen lunches. Apparently the ghosts like the food, too. Here, lights turn on and off, employees get pinched, objects move randomly by themselves, and employees report seeing shadows out of the corners of their eyes, as if someone—or something—is lurking.

Sausage, cold-cut sandwiches, Reubens, hot plates, sauerkraut, special Schilo's root beer, and cherry cheesecake make this a hot spot for lunch. Schilo's, which has been serving customers since 1917, is open for breakfast, lunch, and dinner Monday through Saturday. This deli, located on the upper, or street level, is just a few feet from the river.

SAN ANTONIO ORGANIZED TOURS AND PARANORMAL GROUPS
ALAMO CITY GHOST TOURS
(210) 336-7831
www.alamocityghosttours.com

This ghost-hunting company offers nightly walking tours through downtown San Antonio. According to their website, Alamo City Ghost Tours has been voted by *USA Today* as "one of the best things to do in San Antonio." Tours begin at 9:00 p.m., just across the street from the Alamo, and take visitors on a mile-long route for one and a half hours. While visiting various haunted sites and listening to ghost stories, everyone in the tour group is provided with ghost-hunting equipment, which guides explain how to operate. Tours cost $15 for adults and $10 for children ages five to fourteen.

HAUNTINGS HISTORY OF SAN ANTONIO GHOST HUNT
Alamo Plaza, Alamo Defenders' Monument
San Antonio 78205
(210) 348-6640
www.bestsanantonioghosttours.com

This nightly ghost expedition will lead you on a ninety-minute walking tour of some of the most haunted sites in San

Antonio. Here you can learn about the most recent ghost sightings at the Alamo, Emily Morgan Hotel, Menger Hotel, and other downtown San Antonio locations.

All the guides are also paranormal investigators. Look for the ghost guide with a blue backpack and hat printed with Alamo City Paranormal. Martin Leal started the Alamo City Paranormal ghost-hunting company, which frequently investigates local haunted happenings.

The cost is $15 for ages twelve and up, $10 for children ages six to eleven, and free for children five and younger (be forewarned: The website advertises the tour as "PG-13" and "may not be suitable for young children"). The website has limited information, so you'll need to call the company directly for tour times and other information. The last thirty minutes or so of the tour is devoted to letting tourists search for ghosts using electromagnetic field detectors and temperature sensors.

Leal has special glasses he invented that "charge" the eyes to allow one to see ghosts, which generally appear in a certain range of the color spectrum not visible to the normal human eye. Leal will be happy to let you try them on.

Corpus Christi

Corpus Christi, referred to by locals as the "Sparkling City by the Sea," is located on the South Texas coast. The state's eighth-largest city has the most beautiful bayfront in the state—and a history of hurricanes that have killed hundreds of people.

Here you'll find the spirit of a sailor recounting with pride the engine room where he once worked, the ghost of a world-famous singer who haunts the hotel where she was killed, and an abandoned courthouse haunted by the ghosts of executed prisoners.

Downtown Corpus Christi overlooks a bay of the same name, and luxury homes line the shore along the 13-mile curve from one end of the bayfront to the other. Texas residents have made Corpus Christi and the nearby barrier islands one of their favorite vacation destinations.

CORPUS CHRISTI ACCOMMODATIONS
DAYS INN AIRPORT
901 Navigation Boulevard
Corpus Christi 78408
(361) 888-8599
www.daysinn.com

This hotel in the city's industrial section is said to be haunted by the ghost of the young slain Tejano singer Selena Quintanilla-Perez, who died in 1995 at the hands of her former fan club president after a dispute involving missing money.

The ghost hunters in the Corpus Christi Paranormal club say on their website (www.ccspookcentral.com) that she lingers near the doorway of the room where she was shot and at the hospital (Spohn Memorial) where she was taken after the shooting. They say that motel guests report hearing faint singing and the smell of roses followed by an overwhelming feeling of sorrow. The motel has tried to downplay this bleak part of its history. You're not likely to get much out of the staff unless you're a paying customer.

The motel is 4 miles from Corpus Christi International Airport. There's an outdoor courtyard, playground, and swimming pool. You'll also find laundry facilities, a hotel restaurant, in-room refrigerator and microwave, and free breakfast and Wi-Fi.

Holiday Inn Emerald Beach
1102 South Shoreline
Corpus Christi 78401
(361) 883-5731
www.hotelemeraldbeach.com/default-en.html

This 368-room Holiday Inn is located on the Corpus Christi Bayfront near downtown tourist attractions and many of the city's haunted destinations. It's also the only hotel in downtown Corpus Christi to have its own beach.

McGee Beach is open to the public. You can sit outside and enjoy the view of the bay while sipping drinks brought to you by the hotel waitstaff. The beach is small, but the sand is soft and clean. The hotel is close to several downtown restaurants, including P.F. Chang's and Garibaldi's Pizzeria.

Amenities include an indoor pool, sauna, whirlpool, and play area. Rooms come with a work area, tea and coffeemakers, high-speed Wi-Fi, cable/satellite TV, and a free morning newspaper.

OMNI CORPUS CHRISTI HOTEL MARINA TOWER
707 North Shoreline Boulevard
Corpus Christi 78401
(361) 887-1600
www.omnihotels.com

This Omni sits on Shoreline Boulevard overlooking the Corpus Christi Bayfront. The Omni Marina and its sister, the Omni Bayfront (nearby at 900 North Shoreline Boulevard, 361-880-6738), have 821 guest rooms and suites and three restaurants. The Omni Marina is home to Coastline Cafe Restaurant, serving American cuisine, while the Omni Bayfront is home to the Glass Pavilion Restaurant (steaks, seafood, and pasta) and Republic of Texas Bar and Grill. The Republic of Texas is the only AAA four-diamond restaurant in South Texas. It's by far the best restaurant of the three, but it's pricey. For a good meal at a more reasonable price, try the Glass Pavilion.

You'll find gift shops, swimming pools, fitness centers, and in-house massage therapists. The rooms are top-notch, with twice-daily housekeeping service, work areas, plush robes, evening turndown service, and free Wi-Fi. The Omni is a few blocks from the haunted Nueces County Courthouse and a few more blocks from Heritage Park.

RADISSON ON THE BAY
3200 Surfside Boulevard
Corpus Christi 78402
(361) 883-9700
www.radisson.com

This six-story hotel is located on Corpus Christi Beach just across the Harbor Bridge from downtown. The bridge spans the Corpus Christi ship channel. Two popular tourist attractions—

the Texas State Aquarium and the haunted USS *Lexington* (a decommissioned aircraft carrier)—are located here.

The Radisson has a swimming pool with a poolside cabana bar, hot tub, fitness center, and free high-speed Wi-Fi. The Blue Bay Grill offers a panoramic bay view. Pizza and cocktails are also available in other parts of the hotel.

CORPUS CHRISTI ATTRACTIONS

DEL MAR COLLEGE EAST CAMPUS
101 Baldwin Boulevard
Corpus Christi 78404
www.delmar.edu

The main campus of this community college near Corpus Christi's downtown is said to be haunted by unknown ghosts. Not the whole campus, mind you, just one room in one building—and it just happens to be the oldest building on campus.

Room 222 in the Memorial Classroom Building is believed to be haunted, perhaps by the ghost of a former student who met his or her demise before graduating. Or perhaps it's the ghost of a former professor who "retired" long before he intended.

Whatever the reason, late-night custodial workers and security personnel have reported hearing howls and laughter coming from the room. On one occasion, a security guard heard the sounds of furniture being moved, although he found no evidence to suggest that actually had happened. Perhaps the ghost didn't like the seating arrangements.

HERITAGE PARK
1581 North Chaparral Street
Corpus Christi 78401
(361) 883-0639
http://ccparkandrec.com/government/parks-recreation/
programs-services/arts-culture/index

Heritage Park is a perfect setting for ghosts. The park is composed of nine historical homes that have been moved here,
restored, and converted into office space for nonprofits and
meeting venues for community events.

Corpus Christi Paranormal (www.ccspookcentral.com)
members have compiled an impressive list of ghosts who are
said to haunt these homes. One resides in the Sidbury House,
where a child is said to haunt the children's room, playing
with dolls and moving and knocking things down.

The Galvan House is home to a spirit who taps people on
the shoulder when they visit the second floor. Visitors also
say they've heard footsteps going toward the attic. The ghost
in the Ward-McCampbell House has a name, Mary. Mary, who
supposedly died of pneumonia, likes to make noise. She also
tries to keep the tour guides from entering the house or locks
them out when they venture onto the patio.

Heritage Park is open for free tours Tuesday through Friday each week.

OLD NUECES COUNTY COURTHOUSE
Located on I-37 near the bayfront in Corpus Christi
901 Leopard Street
Corpus Christi 78401
(361) 888-0444

Construction began on this imposing Classical Revival structure
in 1914. The courthouse, like others built in the olden days,
had jail cells on the upper floors. Many who passed through
the court system met their fate at the end of a dangling rope.

The courthouse reportedly had gallows both inside and
out, although a former jailer told the South Texas Paranormal
Society that the indoor gallows was used only once.

The jailer also reported sounds and shadows in the entrance hallway and footsteps coming from a door leading from the kitchen. Kitchen workers reported a cold area near the entrance, a cloudy area near the ceiling, and unexplained drafts that would extinguish burners.

The courthouse is not open to the public. Call to make special arrangements to visit the site free of charge. It's advisable to call well in advance of your visit so a volunteer from the Nueces County Historical Society can arrange to give you a tour. In an interesting development, Corpus Christi Spook Central (www.ccspookcentral.com) has been given permission to investigate the courthouse.

TEXAS STATE AQUARIUM
2710 North Shoreline Boulevard
Corpus Christi 78402
(361) 881-1200 or (800) 477-GULF (4853)
www.texasstateaquarium.org

The Texas State Aquarium is dedicated to educating visitors about the creatures living in the Gulf of Mexico. It overlooks Corpus Christi Bay, the USS *Lexington,* downtown Corpus Christi, and the Corpus Christi ship channel.

The main attraction here is the 132,000-gallon tank with its 35-foot-long acrylic viewing window. Known as the "Islands of Steel" exhibit, this monstrous tank is home to nurse sharks, a giant grouper, and a variety of smaller fish. Another popular attraction is Dolphin Bay, a 400,000-gallon pool featuring dolphins that perform throughout the day. The aquarium, which is open year-round, is built on stilts to prevent flooding during hurricanes. The inside is dimly lit to enhance viewing. The aquarium includes a gift shop, sandwich shop, and bookstore. Admission ranges from $13.95 to

$23.95 (purchase tickets online for best prices); it's free for children two and younger. Parking is $5.00.

USS LEXINGTON
2914 North Shoreline Boulevard
Corpus Christi 78402
(361) 888-4873 or (800) LADY-LEX (523-9539)
www.usslexington.com

Be on the lookout for a young man dressed in a white summer U.S. Navy uniform when you tour this decommissioned aircraft carrier. The polite young man with blond hair and blue eyes enjoys giving visitors a tour of the engine room. He is distinguishable by a slight limp to his left leg. He also has one other distinguishing characteristic: He's a ghost. At least that's the speculation among staffers on this floating museum, who, along with visitors, have spotted the young man or felt his presence from time to time.

People have reported all sorts of odd occurrences, like the time a painting crew returned from a break to find the job finished, or the time a cafe employee felt an invisible *something* trying to push her aside.

Perhaps no one will ever know for sure why this seaman's spirit haunts the *Lexington* and how he met his untimely death. Was he the victim of a Japanese torpedo that struck the carrier on December 4, 1943, or did he die a year later during a kamikaze attack that killed forty-nine people?

Come aboard and see for yourself. Admission is $9.95 for children ages four to twelve, $12.95 for seniors and military, and $14.95 for everyone else; it includes a 3D large-format movie. Parking is $3.50, and doors are open every day except Thanksgiving and Christmas.

WILSON TOWER
606 North Carancahua Street
Corpus Christi 78476
(361) 884-8853

Tenants say the tower is haunted by Mrs. Wilson, who hosted society functions in the penthouse. The elevator stops, the doors open—but no one is there. Or are they? Tenants in this downtown office building report getting a creepy feeling that someone is riding the elevator with them even though they're alone. They also report seeing shadows and hearing sounds while alone in their offices. Occurrences are more common in the early morning hours or late at night.

The SpookCentral.com website (www.ccspookcentral.com) says it may be the ghost of Mrs. Wilson, who once lived with her husband in a four-floor penthouse atop this twenty-one-story office building. The twentieth floor was used as a game room, with a private bar constructed out of mahogany and trimmed in brass and tufted leather. The view from the penthouse was described as rivaling that of the Top of the Mark Restaurant in San Francisco, known for its spectacular view of the city.

CORPUS CHRISTI RESTAURANTS
BLACK BEARD'S ON THE BEACH
3117 East Surfside Boulevard
Corpus Christi 78402
(361) 884-1030
http://blackbeardsrestaurant.net/

The sounds of pots and pans clanging in the kitchen have been reported here. That's not so odd until you consider that the sounds can be heard even when the kitchen is empty. Some employees report seeing the ghostly figure of a woman who is believed to be a former staff member who lost a piece of jewelry in a fire and died trying to retrieve it.

Moving chairs, roving cold spots, and jumping salt shakers have also been reported at this seafood restaurant on Corpus Christi Beach. Other ghosts include that of a man killed in a fight and the ghost of a man who committed suicide nearby after his wife passed away.

This isn't a large or fancy restaurant. You might even feel a little claustrophobic. Booths and tables are crowded into this place. But calm your nerves long enough to order some shrimp—boiled and fried are both good.

KATZ 21 STEAK & SPIRITS
5702 Spohn Drive
Corpus Christi 78401
(361) 884-5289
www.katz21.com

Located on the southside, Katz 21 is a traditional steak house specializing in dry-aged, corn-fed Midwestern prime. The beef is trimmed to the restaurant's specifications, packed, and shipped from Chicago.

Katz's menu also includes seafood, pasta, veal, lamb, and a variety of salads and vegetables. The lunch menu is simpler and less expensive. You can get things like a Philly cheesesteak, a sirloin burger, or french fries at lunch, along with an assortment of soups and salads.

MAMA MIA'S
128 North Mesquite Street
Corpus Christi 78401
(361) 883-3773

Skeptics shook their head when Mama Mia's opened in downtown Corpus Christi back in the early 1990s. Downtown was dead in those days, and the Mesquite Street location didn't exactly give the restaurant panache.

But never underestimate the appeal of good food. The restaurant's Italian owner and main chef, Marino Delzotto, serves up a great assortment of pastas topped with a variety of sauces. Try the pesto pasta. The atmosphere here is warm and cozy with low lighting and the sounds of a boisterous kitchen staff floating through the air.

WATER STREET MARKET
300 block North Water Street
Corpus Christi 78401
(361) 882-8696
www.waterstmarketcc.com/#home-1

You couldn't leave Water Street off a list of recommended restaurants in Corpus Christi even if you wanted to—especially now that it's expanded to three restaurants: The Oyster Bar, Seafood Bar, and Executive Surf Club. Water Street has been serving the best seafood in town for more than twenty years, and now you can satisfy your hunger for a burger and beer at the Surf Club. Belly up to the Oyster Bar for fresh-shucked oysters, or for a fine-dining experience, treat yourself to an elegant dinner at the Seafood Bar, where the immaculately presented fresh seafood almost looks too good to eat. Start your dinner off with pecan-crusted fried oysters, try the signature gulf shrimp and oysters wrapped in bacon, and satisfy your sweet tooth with simply sublime cheesecake. Dress at all three establishments is nice-but-casual, and the service is first rate.

CORPUS CHRISTI ORGANIZED TOURS AND PARANORMAL GROUPS

CORPUS CHRISTI SPOOK CENTRAL

www.ccspookcentral.com

This group of believers is dedicated to the research and study of the paranormal. The volunteer ghost hunters visit haunted sites on a regular basis and will perform a survey of any property believed to be haunted. They take their work seriously and never charge for their services.

Corpus Christi Spook Centraltakes applications via the website. Enrollment is open to anyone, but they claim to pick only "the best." They define "the best" as "individuals that will take research very seriously, have a knack for details and a drive for explaining the unexplainable."

SOUTH TEXAS PARANORMAL SOCIETY

www.southtexasparanormalsociety.com

Much like their friends above, the South Texas Paranormal Society is interested in gathering evidence of the existence of ghosts. They also conduct ghost hunts and have posted their findings on their website.

Victoria

Like many communities in South Texas, Victoria owes its existence to the Spanish and Mexican governments. In 1824, the Mexican government granted permission to Martin De León to establish a settlement between the Guadalupe and Lavaca Rivers. He called it Nuestra Señora Guadalupe de Jésus Victoria.

American settlers later shortened the name to Victoria. Victoria touts itself as "The Crossroads" because of its equidistant location between Houston, San Antonio, Corpus Christi, and Austin.

Here you'll find a haunted movie theater where the ghost likes to call out the names of patrons. You'll also find a park where two ghosts have been seen walking together, and a spooky old courthouse where glowing orbs of light have been spotted in the sky.

VICTORIA ACCOMMODATIONS

Forrest Place Corporate Suites
507 West Forrest Street
Victoria 77901
(361) 578-4260 or (888) 578-4260
www.forrestplace.com

Don't let the name dissuade you: You can stay here even if you're just in town for pleasure. Choose between a pink two-story home or a comfortable bungalow. The one-bedroom suites feature a bath, kitchen, and living area while the two-bedroom suites have one and a half baths, a living room, a kitchen, and a dining area. All suites have Internet access, private phones, and cable television.

Touting itself as "Victoria's Finest Hotel Alternative," the corporate suites come with queen-size bed, kitchen utensils, and modern appliances. Guest laundry facilities are on-site, and housekeeping service is available. The corporate suites are run more like a hotel than a bed-and-breakfast, although the business office is in a separate location.

FRIENDLY OAKS BED AND BREAKFAST
210 East Juan Linn Street
Victoria 77901
(361) 575-0000
www.bedandbreakfast.com/tx-victoria-friendly-oaks.html

The Friendly Oaks is named for the huge live oak trees that grow all around it. Built in 1915, this B&B is located in the historic "Street of Ten Friends" district, named for the families of ten early settlers who built homes close together.

Bill and CeeBee McLeod are friendly folks who will do what they can to make your stay a pleasant one, first greeting you with refreshments upon arrival between 4:00 and 6:00 p.m. Enjoy afternoon tea, dessert, fruit, and nonalcoholic beverages during your stay. Diet, low-fat, vegetarian, and gluten-free meals are available.

Their signature dish is Royal Scottish Pancakes—thin pancakes covered in syrup containing orange and lemon juice, brown sugar, butter, and Drambuie. Pancakes are accompanied by English banger sausages.

Antiques shops, the new Performing Arts Center, and other city attractions such as the Texas Zoo and the haunted Victoria County Courthouse are nearby.

THE INN ON MAIN
315 North Main Street
Victoria 77901
(361) 580-2794
www.the-inn-on-main.com

This bed-and-breakfast was built in 1875 and rescued from the wrecking ball by the Victoria Preservation Society. The society donated it to the original owners, who restored and modernized it.

The inn, which opened in 1998, has four private suites with sitting room, bedroom, and bathroom. Hardwood floors and accents, attractive decor, and a shaded porch make this a perfect place to relax. Suites come with telephones with their own numbers and answering machines. You'll also find combination televisions/VCRs with remote control in each suite. A serve-yourself continental breakfast includes hot and cold drinks, bagels, juice, and fresh fruit.

Next to the inn, the carriage house has been fully renovated into a one-bedroom cottage that is ideal for extended stays. It includes a full bath, a fully equipped kitchen, and a comfortable living room complete with television and fireplace.

The same owners have renovated six other properties in the area, which are available for extended stays as well. Check out the website for information on rates and locations.

LONE STAR INN & SUITES
1907 U.S. Highway 59 North
Victoria 77905
(361) 579-0225
www.hotelinvictoriatx.com

Located on one of the major roads through town, the Lone Star Inn is not far from downtown and several nearby restaurants. Smoking and nonsmoking rooms are available, and rooms come with a king-size bed and pullout sofa or a double queen with breakfast table.

You'll find basic amenities here, such as a coffeemaker, hair dryer, and a free newspaper, as well as an outdoor pool, a barbecue patio, free Wi-Fi, an indoor fitness center, and microwave ovens and small refrigerators in the rooms. The business center is equipped with a fax and copy machine, phone, and computer with high-speed Internet access. This is a nice motel with the basic comforts. It's a good place for those who will be spending most of their time out and about looking for orbs down at the county courthouse or strolling Hopkins Park looking for the ghosts who are said to visit the park at night.

VICTORIA ATTRACTIONS
HOPKINS PARK
505 South Laurent Street
Victoria 7790
(361) 485-3200

Why did the ghost cross the playground? To get to the other slide.

A man is said to have decapitated his girlfriend in the early 1990s on the slide of the playground at this 11.58-acre park, one of the largest in Victoria. The park is home to play equipment, one full basketball court, several picnic tables, and a pavilion.

Residents who live near the park say they have occasionally seen two ghostly figures that appear to be a man and a woman walking through the park.

THE TEXAS ZOO
110 Memorial Drive
Victoria 77901
(361) 573-7681
www.texaszoo.org

The Texas Zoo features more than 150 animals native to Texas, such as the armadillo, Texas river otter, prairie dog, and bald eagle. The property, which covers over six acres, is located inside Riverside Park. The Texas Animal Kingdom Building is home to Texas birds, reptiles, and small mammals, such as red wolves, margay (a type of wild cat), and coati (a member of the raccoon family). You'll also find black bears, red wolves, and jaguarondis, among many other native species. Animals are housed in pens that mimic their natural habitats. Children will enjoy both the animals and the playground. Admission is $7 for adults, $5.50 for seniors, and $6 for active/retired military and for children ages three to twelve.

Since 2012 the Texas Zoo has hosted a Haunted Zoo over Halloween weekend. It runs from 8:00 p.m. to midnight and is composed of more than a hundred volunteers who wear frightfully convincing costumes and convert the zoo into a terrifying landscape full of scary surprises. The event has become so popular that attendance is in the thousands, so get in line early for your $10 tickets.

VICTORIA COUNTY COURTHOUSE
115 North Bridge Street
Victoria 77901
(361) 575-4558
www.vctx.org

This is another one of those places that looks like it should be haunted. The historic courthouse, built in 1892, is located in the center of town.

Over the years, construction workers and courthouse employees claim to have seen moving flashes of light around the outside of the building. They've also reported an apparition that shows up on the second floor in the southeast corner. Perhaps it's the ghost of the architect, J. Riely Gordon, who was fired for not living up to his contract, which required him to be present each day that construction took place.

Featuring Romanesque architecture, with its heavy masonry, round arches, and simple ornamentation, this imposing structure is made of Texas granite and Indiana limestone. The clock in the tower still strikes on the hour. A renovation in 1967 restored and modernized the building.

VICTORIA RESTAURANTS
Double J Eatery
8607 North Navarro Street
Victoria 77904
(361) 570-7744
www.doublejeatery.com

Double J Eatery is a great place for hamburgers and daily lunch specials; in 2016, locals voted its hand-cut and hand-dipped chicken-fried steaks the best in Victoria for the third year in a row. The casual-dining restaurant is busiest at lunch.

Dinner is served in a more relaxed atmosphere, with modern corrugated tin walls and a bar covered with rustic western accents. The Double J is open Monday through Saturday for lunch and dinner.

FOSSATI'S DELICATESSEN
302 South Main Street
Victoria 77901
(361) 576-3354

Victoria residents have been heading to Fossati's for great deli sandwiches since 1882. That's right: 1882. Any restaurant that's been open that long must be good. Fossati's, run by the Fossati family, is the oldest delicatessen in Texas.

Along with sandwiches, you'll find soups, salads, and Italian entrees on the menu. Try the Reuben sandwich, a cup of minestrone, the spaghetti, or the homemade lasagna. Fossati's is open for lunch Monday through Friday. Here you'll find a good mix of tourists and locals in a casual-yet-lively atmosphere.

TOSCANA ARTISAN BAKERY & BISTRO
6322 North Navarro Street
Victoria 77904
(361) 579-9597

This combination bakery, pizzeria, and fine-dining restaurant is a bit of an oddity in Victoria. If you didn't know any better, you'd think you were in Houston or Dallas. That's how good the food is. The main feature of this relatively new restaurant is the wood-fired oven. Almost everything made here either starts out or ends up in the oven, giving a pleasant grilled flavor to the selections.

Dine indoors, in the garden courtyard, or in one of two private dining rooms. Toscana is open daily for breakfast, lunch, and dinner. The atmosphere is warm and cozy with the perpetual odor of grilled food in the air.

VICTORIA ORGANIZED TOURS
AND PARANORMAL GROUPS

Paranormal Organization of South Texas
http://parasouthtx.com

This informal group of ghost hunters can be contacted through its website. Cofounders Brian and Andy and other paranormal investigators investigate haunted sites simply for fun, not for profit. They don't accept money for their investigations. They will, however, ask for gas money if you live more than 35 miles away. So far, the group has investigated private residences, cemeteries, the old Nueces County Courthouse, and Heritage Park. Membership is free and open to anyone interested in paranormal investigations. To join, contact Brian and Andy using the "Contact P.O.S.T." link on their website.

SOUTH TEXAS DAY TRIPS
AND GETAWAY WEEKENDS

The town of Goliad would be worth a day trip or weekend getaway even if it weren't haunted. But tales of the spirits of 300 executed Texans roaming a fort located here makes it even more attractive to ghost hunters and worth the short drive from Corpus Christi, San Antonio, or Victoria. The fact that visitors can spend the night in the fort makes it all the better.

The Texas Revolution began in Goliad on October 9, 1835, when colonists captured the fort and town. The Texas Declaration of Independence was signed in Goliad on December 20, 1835, and the first Texas flag (featuring a drawing of a severed, bloody arm) flew above the fort. The fort later became the site of the "Goliad Massacre," when Mexican general Santa Anna ordered the execution of Colonel James Walker Fannin Jr. and his men.

The fort, known as **Presidio La Bahia,** is a National Historic Landmark and dates back to the 1700s. It and the nearby

Mission Espíritu Santo are the only Spanish colonial fort and museum complexes in the Western Hemisphere. The presidio (the Spanish word for "fort") is operated by the Catholic Diocese of Victoria as a museum with historic artifacts, gift shop, and sleeping quarters.

It's not surprising that this stone fort is haunted. Despite having surrendered, Fannin and his 300 men were executed on Palm Sunday, March 27, 1836. Visitors have reported hearing moans and sighs in the courtyard. Are these the spirits of the men who were killed for daring to challenge Mexican authority? Other paranormal phenomena include a woman who is seen praying in the chapel, a 4-foot-tall friar who roams the adjacent chapel yard, and a cold and misty area in one corner of that yard.

In her book *Haunted Texas Vacations*, Lisa Farwell quotes a newspaper article about a security guard named Jim Leos Jr., who spent a terrifying night at the fort back in the early 1990s. He reported hearing the shrill cries of what he estimated to be a dozen or so terrified infants. He later heard the sound of a women's choir coming from the back wall of the fort. The aforementioned friar appeared in front of the chapel later that night before wandering the grounds for what Leos estimated to be an hour or more.

In 2000 the ghost-investigating group known as Lone Star Spirits also spent a frightening night there. One investigator reported the "smell of death" in the southeast corner of the quadrangle (the name given to the area inside the fort's four walls), while others reported seeing a "strange, thick mist" in that area later in the night. A microphone placed inside the oversize keyhole to the locked chapel door picked up the sounds of furniture being moved inside and a voice recording of someone saying, "Doesn't fit."

The crew wound up sleeping in their cars because someone—or *something*—kept banging on one of the doors to their sleeping quarters, and one shaken investigator felt his bed rising off the floor. They also reported the sound of a galloping horse, strange mumblings, and seeing a "humanoid shadow" moving behind the well in the quadrangle. You can read their entire report at www.lsspi.org.

The Mission Espíritu Santo sits across the river in the 2,208-acre **Goliad State Historical Park.** The mission, established in 1749, is home to several interpretive displays. It's also home to the ghost of a Native American on horseback. Witnesses claim to have heard the sound of drums and the smell of tobacco burned in a peace pipe. Others report seeing a phantom wolf that runs into the woods and disappears.

Along with the mission and fort, the city is home to the **General Zaragoza State Historic Site.** This state park is the site of the reconstructed birthplace and statue of General Ignacio Zaragoza (1829–1862). Zaragoza was a Mexican Revolutionary hero who defeated a superior French army in defense of the Central Mexico city of Puebla. The battle date, Cinco de Mayo (May 5), is a national holiday in Mexico and celebrated throughout Texas.

Another Goliad monument marks the **grave** (2 miles south of Goliad off U.S. Highway 183) of the executed Colonel Fannin and his troops. The monument, a few hundred yards from Presidio La Bahia, is the site of memorial services each year near the weekend of March 27. Fannin Plaza, a city park on South Market and Franklin Streets, features a cannon from the Texas Revolution and several historical markers.

The city's "hanging tree," the majestic 1894 courthouse, and **Market House Museum** (at Franklin and Market Streets) can be found nearby. The museum houses historic artifacts and overlooks the town square, which has been lovingly restored. The square is the site of the **Goliad Market Days,** held on the second Saturday of each month, featuring food, art, and crafts, along with the usual antiques, clothing, and collectibles offered by merchants in the square's historic buildings.

At the end of Market Street is the almost 2-mile-long **Angel of Goliad Hike/Bike/Nature Trail,** which connects the town square with Goliad State Park and Presidio La Bahia. The trail is named for Panchita Alvarez, the wife of a high-ranking officer in the Mexican Army, who begged the commanding officer to spare the lives of Fannin and his men and is credited with saving twenty-eight souls.

The secluded trail follows the banks of the San Antonio River, ultimately winding its way to the graves of Colonel Fannin and his soldiers. Interpretive signs point to mulberry, mesquite, hackberry, and palmetto trees, among others, along with vines that go by names like saw greenbrier, mustang grape, and southern dewberry.

Take a step back in time without giving up modern amenities when you stay in **The Quarters at Presidio La Bahia.** This former commander's quarters greets you with thick, wooden doors, rock walls, ceiling timbers, and polished floor pavers. A family of four can easily fit into this two-bedroom suite adjacent to the Presidio La Bahia Museum. Guests enter through private entrances leading from the presidio's courtyard and the front parking lot, providing a private enclave in the midst of a working museum.

The suite comes with a living room, dining area, bathroom, and kitchenette. The master bedroom offers a queen-size bed, and a second bedroom is furnished with twin beds. Historical paintings and antique light fixtures decorate the rooms, along with silk flower arrangements and rustic wood-and-leather furniture. Modern amenities like a running shower, toilet, refrigerator, stove, and oven have been added. You'll also find dishes, cutlery, mugs, glasses, two coffeemakers, pots, and pans. You will not, however, find a television. A telephone is connected to the museum's telephone line, so the ringer has been turned off and the phone is to be used only in emergencies.

But who needs telephones and televisions? Silence is the primary amenity offered at The Quarters—a silence that falls over this ancient fort once the museum closes. Presidio La Bahia is 1 mile south of Goliad on US 183. It costs around $160 a night on weekends. Make arrangements early by calling (361) 645-3752. You can view The Quarters at www.presidiola bahia.org/quarters.htm.

You don't have to go hungry in Goliad, although you'll find your choices limited. Truly fine dining is unavailable, and most restaurants fall either into the category of fast-food chains (Dairy Queen and Whataburger) or privately owned hole-in-the-wall establishments.

Of course, good food can be found in all sorts of unexpected places. You may find, though, that you have to drive 20 or 30 miles to find a good restaurant. You'll have enough choices here to skip the fast food, although you may find yourself visiting the same restaurant more than once if you stay two or more days.

Mattie's Bakery and Café (103 South Courthouse Square, 361-405-2077) is located on Goliad's historic square. It's open for breakfast, lunch, and early dinner, and the coffee and cinnamon rolls get rave reviews. Check out the lunch special or soup of the day, and don't even try to walk past the tempting display of fresh-baked pies and pastries without satisfying your sweet tooth.

Blue Quail Deli (224 South Commercial Street, 361-645-1600, www.bluequaildeli.com) is located on the west side of Goliad's Market Square. But don't dawdle; it's only open for lunch. Sit at the window and look out at the town square. Try the Not-so-Poor Boy (roast beef, ham, smoked turkey, and cheddar cheese served with mustard and mayo on a sub roll). The homemade cobbler may be the best item on the menu.

RIO GRANDE VALLEY

Brownsville

Brownsville's motto says it best: "On the border by the sea." This city of approximately 183,000 is just across the border from Matamoros, Mexico, and a short drive from South Padre Island, which attracts beach-loving tourists, including a sizable population during spring break.

Brownsville, with the rest of the Rio Grande Valley, is located in a semitropical area filled with exotic birds and plants. The city's proximity to Mexico gives it an international feel. The largest city in the Rio Grande Valley, Brownsville was founded on January 13, 1849.

The city's ghosts include Civil War soldiers—and phantom cows.

BROWNSVILLE ACCOMMODATIONS

COURTYARD BY MARRIOTT

3955 North Expressway 77/83
Brownsville 78520
(956) 350-4600
www.marriott.com

This eighty-room, three-suite hotel is located on the main road into Brownsville. You're not likely to miss it unless you arrive by plane or by country road. The Courtyard by Marriott is modern, cozy, and very attractive.

A swimming pool, hot tub, exercise room, restaurant, and bar are located on-site. Sit outside on the covered patio and enjoy a drink with friends. The Courtyard's restaurant serves a hot breakfast buffet each morning along with cooked-to-order selections.

Rooms come with wired and wireless high-speed Internet access. And don't worry, it's free. You'll also find a large desk with an ergonomic chair in your room, along with a speaker phone, voice mail, dataports, hair dryer, iron/ironing board, in-room coffee/tea, and cable TV. Suites include a separate living room with room for six, a microwave, a refrigerator, and a balcony overlooking a courtyard and swimming pool.

The Courtyard by Marriott is not far from the Gladys Porter Zoo, the Port of Brownsville, the haunted Fort Brown, and the U.S./Mexico border.

HOMEWOOD SUITES BY HILTON
3759 North Expressway
Brownsville 78520
(956) 574-6900
http://homewoodsuites3.hilton.com

Homewood Suites is just off the North Expressway, more formally known as U.S. Highway 77/83. It's also located across the street from Brownsville's Sunrise Mall, where you'll find major department stores, specialty shops, and a food court.

This all-suite hotel gives you the option of a studio, one-bedroom, or two-bedroom suite equipped with kitchens outfitted with dishes, pots, pans, utensils, and a central living area. You can dine in one of the many nearby restaurants. The hotel also provides a complimentary breakfast buffet every morning along with a light dinner and drinks Monday through Thursday.

Hotel amenities include an outdoor swimming pool, hot tub, barbecue area, and basketball court. Wireless Internet access is available in all rooms, along with cable TV.

STAYBRIDGE SUITES
2900 Pablo Kiesel Boulevard
Brownsville 78526
(956) 504-9500
www.staybridge.com

Staybridge personnel refer to this as an "all-suite, extended-stay hotel that caters to guests looking for temporary housing." The fact is, anyone can stay here, and it's a good deal when you consider all the space and amenities you get.

Suites feature full kitchens, a warm decor, and enough space to make you feel at home—even when you're on vacation. You'll find an exercise room and a lounge where you can relax, talk, or read. It's sort of like a lobby but without all the coming-and-going traffic.

The Staybridge Suites are located in the Sunrise Commons shopping center north of the Mexican city of Matamoros and just east of the Brownsville/South Padre Island International Airport. It's also only a short drive from the Rio Grande and Fort Brown, which is haunted by several spirits.

BROWNSVILLE ATTRACTIONS

FARM ROAD 511
Brownsville lays claim as the only city in the world to have phantom cows. They're said to roam Farm Road 511, a stretch of road in southern Brownsville that is also known as Senator Eddie Lucio Jr. Highway. It forms an outer loop or bypass of the main portion of the city.

These shadowy bovines pop up in front of vehicles late at night and then disappear as quickly as they appeared. Several car accidents have been attributed to them. Drivers involved

The Little Boy of Fort Brown

Fort Brown served an important role in U.S. and Texas history. It now sits on the campus of the University of Texas at Brownsville and Texas Southmost College. The campus is bisected by two *resacas* (lagoons) that add a touch of beauty to the area.

The resacas also play a pivotal role in one of the ghost encounters experienced by campus regulars as well as occasional visitors. The story varies in detail from person to person, but common threads emerge when the versions are examined.

The story is recounted in *The Ghosts of Fort Brown: An Informal Study of Brownsville Folklore and Parapsychology*, published in 2003 by the Arnulfo L. Oliveira Literary Society (http://blue.utb.edu/ghostsoffortbrown). A synopsis of the story goes something like this: It begins at dusk on a warm day as you walk near one of the resacas. You spot a little boy with dark hair and dark eyes playing all alone. He skips and jumps and throws stones in the water, oblivious to your presence.

Then, at a certain point and for no apparent reason, the boy notices you and draws near. Soaking wet and barefooted, he takes your hand. His hand is cold. He is dressed in a white silk shirt like those worn in the late nineteenth and early twentieth centuries, black velvet shorts, and white stockings.

He asks you to lift him and swing him through the air. He is a sweet little boy who nonetheless ignores you when you try to engage him in conversation. Some say he speaks English, others say he speaks Spanish. Whatever the language, the message is always the same.

"Tell my mother I am safe," he says. "She is crying. Please tell her I'm OK. Please make her stop crying."

The boy eventually lets go of you and skips down the street, and as the sun goes down and darkness descends, the boy simply disappears into the darkness, never to be seen again. Some speculate that the boy drowned in one of the lagoons and his body was never found. His mother, they say, searches for him to this day, and the boy is concerned that his mother is still worried for his safety.

So don't be surprised if you encounter a small boy someday while walking along the resacas. And if you do, please reassure him that his mother is all right.

in the accidents, however, have found no signs of the culpable cows, not even a patty to prove them right.

Many have described this experience as "udderly" strange.

FORT BROWN, UNIVERSITY OF TEXAS AT BROWNSVILLE/ TEXAS SOUTHMOST COLLEGE
80 Fort Brown Street
Brownsville 78520
(956) 544-8200

Fort Brown began as nothing more than a bit of dirt shaped from the banks of the Rio Grande shortly after the U.S./Mexican War broke out in 1846. The fort was moved a short distance, and through the years was destroyed and rebuilt three times. Both Union and Confederate soldiers occupied the fort at various times during the Civil War. It now sits on the University of Texas at Brownsville/Texas Southmost College campus.

Referred to as the "Fort Brown Zone" by university officials, this area of the campus is said to be haunted by apparitions of Civil War soldiers, horses, and battlefield noises. Some have reported hearing the sounds of explosions (or perhaps cannon fire) and men screaming.

The building that served as a morgue during the Civil War is believed to be haunted by a woman and her child, although no one is quite sure whether the child is a boy or a girl. Another woman, dressed in black, appears on the outside steps. Other spirits knock books from shelves, create electrical disturbances, unplug appliances, and move things around, such as chairs, wastebaskets, and pens and pencils.

GLADYS PORTER ZOO
500 Ringgold Street
Brownsville 78520
(956) 546-2177
www.gpz.org

The Gladys Porter Zoo is widely considered one of the best small zoos in the country. It's situated on twenty-six acres covered in lush tropical vegetation and houses approximately 1,600 animals. The zoo has a good reputation for breeding endangered species.

Visitors can see as many as 377 species of animals and 225 plant varieties. Take a safari through Africa, Asia, Tropical America, and Indo-Australia. Other sites you'll want to visit are the Herpetarium and Aquatic Wing, the Free-Flight Aviary, Macaw Canyon, Bear Grottoes, and an exhibit of California sea lions.

Small World is the zoo's nursery and petting zoo, where children can get up close and personal with domesticated animals like goats and llamas. Many of the zoo's creatures aren't captive at all, but are the many wild birds drawn to the park's plants and water.

The Earl C. Sams Foundation planned, built, stocked, and equipped the zoo before turning it over to the City of Brownsville. Named for one of the Sams daughters, the Gladys Porter Zoo opened on September 3, 1971. The zoo is open year-round. Admission is $11.00 for adults, $9.50 for seniors, $8.00 for children ages two to thirteen, and free for children under two.

PALO ALTO BATTLEGROUND NATIONAL HISTORIC SITE
5 miles north of Brownsville at FM 1847 and FM 511
1623 Central Boulevard, Room 213
Brownsville, 78520
(956) 541-2785
www.nps.gov/paal/index.htm

This historic battlefield commemorates the Battle of Palo Alto, which took place on May 8, 1846, setting off the U.S./Mexican War. It became a National Historic Landmark in 1960 and a National Historic Site in 1978.

The battle between U.S. and Mexican troops was the first in a two-year-long conflict that changed the map of North America. The 3,400-acre site includes a visitor center filled with exhibits that explain the events that took place here and the reasons for the war.

Visitors can view the battlefield from an overlook or hike on one of the many trails.

BROWNSVILLE RESTAURANTS
COBBLEHEADS BAR & GRILL RESTAURANT
3154 Central Boulevard
Brownsville 78520
(956) 546-6224
www.cobbleheads.com

Cobbleheads is located on a busy Brownsville street. You'll recognize it by the green metal roof and red-brick veneer. It looks like a cross between an old-fashioned railway car and one of those modern trolleys you see shuttling tourists around downtowns all over the country.

This restaurant seats more than 150 people in its dining room, bar, and covered patio, which overlooks a pond with a fountain that spews water into the air. The dining room is cozy and a little on the romantic side, with its terrazzo tile, soft lighting, and lots of greenery. It's a bit more casual and open in the bar, and the covered patio can be whatever you make of it.

Cobbleheads serves a range of foods, including steaks, seafood, and sandwiches. Definitely save room for the fried ice cream for dessert.

MADEIRA
805 Media Luna
Brownsville 78520
(956) 504-3100

Given its great number of inexpensive but authentic Mexican eateries, Brownsville isn't known for its upscale restaurants, but this place is worth dressing up for. The menu has something to please everyone, and includes an impressive selection of beer, wine, and mixed drinks. Start with a peppery watercress and goat cheese salad or the sweet and spicy scallop ceviche, then choose from an enticing list of fresh seafood or beef tenderloin entrees. The staff can be trusted to recommend the perfect beverage to complement your dinner. Madeira is open for dinner Monday through Saturday, and you can choose to be seated indoors in the spacious, high-ceiling dining room or outdoors on the covered deck overlooking the resaca.

Laredo

Located on the north bank of the Rio Grande, Laredo was founded in 1755 while still a part of the Spanish colony of New Spain. In 1840 it became the capital of the independent Republic of the Rio Grande, which seceded from Mexico in protest of the dictatorship of Antonio López de Santa Anna.

Laredo is 130 miles west of Corpus Christi and 144 miles southwest of San Antonio. This city of over 250,000 is across the river from Nuevo Laredo, Mexico, which has a population of nearly 374,000. The combined populations and the amount of trade that crosses the bridges between the United States and Mexico here give Laredo a much larger—and more sophisticated—feel from other cities its size.

Local ghosts include a nun, a state trooper, and a mother searching for the three children she pushed off a cliff. Maybe they're hiding from her. Wouldn't you?

LAREDO ACCOMMODATIONS

LA POSADA HOTEL/SUITES
100 Zaragoza Street
Laredo 78040
(956) 722-1701
www.laposadahotel.com

La Posada (Spanish for "The Inn") is the premier hotel in Laredo. Not only is it located near the northern bank of the Rio Grande and between two international bridges, this century-old hotel is steeped in history and offers some of the best amenities in town. It also offers the ghost of a nun at no extra charge.

La Posada began life in the early 1900s as a Spanish colonial convent and, later, as a small hotel. Through the years, it has grown into a full-scale hotel with modern amenities wrapped in Old World charm. The Tack Room Bar & Grill once served as the Old Laredo Telephone Exchange (the phone company), while the Zaragosa Grill offers "upscale bistro dining with a Latin flair." The 150-year-old capitol building of the Republic of the Rio Grande is now an adjacent museum.

The hotel boasts 206 rooms, 57 suites, and 22 concierge-level rooms. Amenities include two outdoor swimming pools (one heated); a fitness center, business center, and gift shop; and complimentary airport shuttle. Rooms come with business-size desks, cable TV, movies, wireless Internet access, in-room safe deposit boxes, coffee service, and room service.

Having once served as a convent, it should come as no surprise that La Posada is haunted by the spirit of a nun. Many have seen her roaming the hotel, although no one has been able to determine what she's looking for. Some have reported a spirit taking the form of employees. These ghostly shape shifters will look at you, but they won't speak.

Other paranormal occurrences include cold spots, the sound of someone calling your name, objects moving and falling for no reason, and the sound of footsteps in the hotel ballroom.

RIALTO HOTEL
1219 Matamoros Street
Laredo 78040
(956) 725-1800
www.therialtohotel.com

This downtown retreat is a refreshing change from the chain hotels found in every American city. The hotel's style is described as "early-twentieth-century Beaux Arts architecture

and design," where "beautiful hallways are accented by brack-
eted tile cornices with modillion friezes." You don't have to be
an architect, however, to enjoy your stay here.

The Rialto is one block from the city's historic center and
a mile from Nuevo Laredo and the Laredo Center for the Arts.
Hotel amenities include an on-site Seattle's Best Coffee, the
Rialto Cafe (serving deli specialties three meals a day), free
lobby newspapers, a fitness center, a business center, and Wi-Fi.
The hotel's forty-nine guest rooms on five floors are furnished in early twentieth-century mahogany pieces. They
come with business-size desks, DirecTV, and high-speed Internet access. Turndown service is available upon request. Each
room comes with coffee, tea, and toiletries.

RIO GRANDE PLAZA HOTEL
1 South Main Avenue
Laredo 78040
(956) 722-2411
www.riograndeplaza.com

This fifteen-story circular building boasts the largest guest
rooms in Laredo. It's located near the Rio Grande next to the
International Bridge. A ten-minute walk will bring you to the
center of Laredo or to dining and shopping in Mexico, or "Old
Mexico," as some people like to call it.

An elevated pool overlooks the river and Nuevo Laredo.
Guests have access to a fitness room, complimentary shuttle
transportation, and free parking. The 195 rooms come with
views of the river or the city. Rooms are equipped with an
alarm clock, radio, iron and ironing board, hair dryer, refrigerator, microwave, coffeemaker, and cable TV. The Rio Grande is
not far from this hotel. Take a drive to the river and see if you
encounter the spirit of Maria, who is said to be searching for
her children (see the Rio Grande entry in Laredo Attractions).

LAREDO ATTRACTIONS

Lamar Bruni Vergara Science Center

5201 University Boulevard
Laredo 78041
(956) 326-2001
www.tamiu.edu/coas/planetarium

The Lamar Bruni Vergara Science Center is an elaborate name for a planetarium built on the campus of Texas A&M International University. The planetarium has one of the few new-generation digital projectors that allow for views from any part of the known universe.

This high-tech system allows visitors to travel to parts of the universe seen before only by astronomers with powerful telescopes. The planetarium's website describes the experience this way: "The Digital 3 projectors use powerful graphics hardware and software to generate immersive full-dome images on the interior surface of a dome, integrating all-dome video, real-time 3D computer graphics, and a complete digital astronomy package."

In other words, it's really cool. If you're somewhat confused, ask your kids or grandkids what all this means. Different shows are held throughout the week, and admission will only set you back $3 to $4 per person.

Laredo Center for the Arts

500 San Agustin Avenue
Laredo 78040
(956) 725-1715
www.laredoartcenter.org

The Laredo Center for the Arts hosts a variety of artistic and cultural events. International art exhibitions, dance recitals, musical performances, and art education classes are held here. The center was founded in 1993 in the former city hall building, an 1880s-era structure located in historic Market Square. The center is home to the Webb County Heritage Foundation as well as a gallery for the Laredo Art League. The Goodman Gallery, the Lilia G. Martinez Gallery, and the Community Gallery are dedicated to displaying works by local artists.

LAREDO HEALTH DEPARTMENT
2600 Cedar Avenue
Laredo 78040
(956) 795-4900

The Laredo Health Department's mission statement reads: "As a leader in public health, the City of Laredo Health Department is committed to providing [a] culturally competent environment for the residents of Laredo." Makes you wonder why the place is haunted. Did someone slack off and inadvertently kill someone? Does the ghost of this unwitting victim haunt the place, making sure health officials do their jobs?

Employees report apparitions roaming the offices after working hours. They look more like shadowy figures than fully formed people. Lights flicker on and off, and janitors report cold spots and eerie feelings. They also say their cleaning supplies often move from one place to another without explanation. You'll have to call and make special arrangements to tour this building after hours.

RIO GRANDE
No one knows for sure where it happened. Somewhere along the Rio Grande a woman named Maria is said to have pushed her three children off a cliff and then plunged to her death from the same cliff the next day.

Locals say that if you visit the river and she sees you, she will sometimes mistake you for her children. According to local lore, Maria comes closer and then, realizing her mistake, vanishes.

THE OFFICE OF J. P. OSCAR MARTINEZ
8501 San Dario
Laredo 78045
(956) 721-2510

Judge Oscar Martinez retired in 2015 as Webb County Precinct Four Justice of the Peace. His former office, now occupied by Jose "Pepe" Salinas, is the site of mysterious activity. The office is in the former Department of Public Safety building. DPS officers are more commonly known as state troopers. Several employees have seen what they believe to be a deceased DPS officer wandering the building.

This spectral trooper turns lights and computers on and off, slams doors, and shuffles papers and files. Employees say they feel a strange sensation of being watched and experience cold chills. Some report seeing doorknobs on closed doors turning slowly, as if someone is preparing to slip into the room. An investigation reveals no one on the other side.

At least, no one who can be seen . . .

LAREDO RESTAURANTS
TACK ROOM BAR & GRILL
100 Zaragoza Street
Laredo 78040
(956) 722-1701
www.tackroomlaredo.com

The Tack Room is located in La Posada Hotel/Suites. Victorian racing decor gives this restaurant its name. Entrees are cooked on a copper-topped grill for everyone to see. Gulf seafood,

Black Angus steaks, baby back ribs, and ostrich burgers are among the favorites here.

Sandwiches, soups, salads, and Mexican food make up the rest of the menu. You might also want to try the portobello mushroom-and-spinach quesadillas. Sauces here are made on-site and include a variety of chiles, not all of which will burn your mouth. Chicken, venison, and quail also are available. The desserts here are traditional—cheesecake, flan, key lime pie, chocolate cake, and carrot cake—but they're made on the premises rather than being brought in from elsewhere.

TACO PALENQUE
7 locations in Laredo
www.tacopalenque.com

Taco Palenque is the most recent invention of the family of Juan Francisco.

"Pancho" Ochoa opened his first roadside chicken stand in Mexico in 1975 and named it El Pollo Loco, Spanish for "The Crazy Chicken." He began serving hand-marinated chicken using a family recipe that included herbs, spices, and citrus juices.

The business took off so fast that four years later, the family had eighty-five restaurants in twenty cities in northern Mexico. The business soon migrated across the border, and in 1983 Denny's bought the El Pollo Loco chain.

Now the Ochoa family has opened Taco Palenque at over twenty sites throughout the state, including several locations in Laredo, New Braunfels, Houston, San Antonio, Edinburg, Brownsville, and elsewhere.

You'll find a wide array of Mexican foods here, with many of the meats flame-broiled like the chicken at El Pollo Loco. Recommendations include fajitas (chicken or beef) with guacamole, carne guisada, or any of the numerous varieties of breakfast tacos. For dessert, try the flan or pineapple empanadas.

McAllen

McAllen is named for John McAllen, one of the city's founders, who established a town site known as West McAllen in 1904. Three years later, other developers began their own town east of West McAllen. Guess what they named it? That's right, East McAllen.

Eventually the two developments grew together and became one town, so residents decided to just call it McAllen. This city 5 miles from the border with Mexico is home now to more than 138,000 people.

McAllen is known as the "City of Palms" for the thousands of palm trees that decorate the landscape and line many city streets. Colorful flowers and exotic birds abound. You'll also find thousands of "snowbirds" during the winter months, when northerners gas up their RVs and head to the Rio Grande Valley to escape the harsh winter weather. Haunted places include a Toys R Us haunted by the spirit of a young boy, a football stadium where a high school girl fell to her death, and a Spanish mission haunted by three priests once stationed there.

McALLEN ACCOMMODATIONS
HILTON GARDEN INN MCALLEN AIRPORT
617 West US 83
McAllen 78501
(956) 664-2900
www.hiltongardeninn.com

This white stucco building with red-tiled roof provides visitors the basics in comfort in an attractive, well-kept package. Hotel amenities include a twenty-four-hour pantry, free business center, swimming pool, and exercise room. Breakfast is served each morning in the Great American Grill, and you can down a cold drink from 5:00 p.m. to 10:00 p.m. at the Great American Grill Lounge.

Room amenities include a sofa bed, adjustable thermostat, cable TV with HBO, video games, and a work desk with adjustable lamp. Other amenities include coffeemakers, refrigerators, high-speed Internet access, and irons and ironing boards. The Hilton Garden is a short drive down U.S. Highway 83 to the haunted La Lomita Mission.

CASA DE PALMAS RENAISSANCE MCALLEN HOTEL
101 North Main Street
McAllen 78501
(956) 631-1101
www.marriott.com

This Texas Historic Landmark, aptly named the House of Palms, is, at last count, surrounded by ninety-two palm trees. You can't miss this historic hotel built in 1918. It's the mission-style building with pink walls and blood-red tile roof.

The hotel has been restored to its original beauty and enhanced with modern amenities. The on-site restaurant, known as the Spanish Room, serves up "classic continental fare with a Latin fusion showcasing the indigenous flavors of South Texas," according to their website. Patio dining and light snacks near the pool also are available.

Hotel amenities include covered parking, gift shop, free safe deposit box, twenty-four-hour exercise room, concierge service, continental breakfast, and a free newspaper delivered to your room. Other amenities include a twenty-four-hour business center, gift shop/newsstand, and laundry valet.

The 165 rooms are beautifully decorated and come with pillow-top mattresses, down pillows, hair dryers, iron and ironing board, and minibars. Other amenities include complimentary soaps and lotions, cable TV, free coffee and tea service, a work area, and high-speed Internet access. The Renaissance is a short drive from the haunted Museum of South Texas History (see McAllen Attractions).

McALLEN ATTRACTIONS

LA LOMITA MISSION

FM 1016, 3 miles south of U.S. Highway 83
Mission 78572
(956) 580-8760

The city of Mission, located 5 miles to the north of McAllen, is named for this haunted site. La Lomita is Spanish for "little hill." The site encompasses a hill, a former mission, and ranch headquarters maintained by the Oblates of Mary Immaculate. The lands here once supported the priests and their charities. The original chapel, built in 1865, has been rebuilt or restored at least twice. It was moved to its current site in 1899.

The Mission Chamber of Commerce isn't going to like this listing. The ghosts associated with this site are said to be the spirits of three priests who once lived at the mission. Legend has it that the priests and nuns forgot their vows of celibacy, and the infants born from their trysts were buried on the mission's grounds.

One night, two unknown assailants attacked the mission, killing two priests and sending the other fleeing for help. The story has it that he, too, died, although it's not known in what manner. No one seems to know what happened to the nuns.

People who have visited the mission report seeing figures in robes walking around the grounds at night. Perhaps they're searching for the burial sites of the infants the priests fathered and then killed.

MISSION HIGH SCHOOL FOOTBALL STADIUM
1802 Cleo Dawson Road
Mission 78572
(956) 323-5700

Mission High School was the only high school in the city for many years. Its population rose to more than 4,000 students before the school district split it in two, creating a second school known as Veterans Memorial High School.

The school's stadium is named for the former coach of the Dallas Cowboys, who grew up in Mission. Tom Landry Stadium hosts football games, graduations, and other public events. It holds more than 30,000 fans—including a young female ghost.

Some say this young girl fell to her death from the top bleachers during a sporting event. Her ghost returns to the bleachers at dusk. Look carefully if you happen to come here during a football game. The young girl sitting near the top of the bleachers may just be a spirit instead of a spirited fan.

MUSEUM OF SOUTH TEXAS HISTORY
121 East McIntyre Street
Edinburg 78541
(956) 383-6911
www.mosthistory.org

This small museum in Edinburg, 5 miles northwest of McAllen, is dedicated to preserving and displaying the blended heritage and culture of the border region of Mexico and Texas. Exhibits include prehistoric plants and animal fossils, a steamboat replica, and artifacts from native people and European colonists.

The museum has been in existence since 1967. It first opened in the old Hidalgo County jail. The museum has since expanded thanks to a $5.5 million addition, although part of the museum is still housed in what once served as the jail building.

People apparently get an eerie feeling in this portion of the museum. It's especially obvious as you climb the stairs to the museum's tower, which once served as the hanging room. Prisoners sentenced to die were hanged from the rafters. Visitors have reported a cold spot in the tower, and others say the hangman's noose that hangs inside the tower can be seen swaying back and forth even when all the doors and windows are closed.

The shadow of a man hanging from a rope has been reported, and some people have reported hearing wailing and moaning coming from the jail area at night.

Toys R Us

1101 West Expressway 83
McAllen 78501
(956) 682-8697

Several years ago, a young boy is reported to have broken his neck after falling from a ladder that a careless employee left standing inside the store. Stockers who work overnight after the store has closed say they've heard the sound of a young boy laughing and running through the store.

Lights go on and off, and locked doors open. It may sound a bit creepy, but look at it this way: Spending an eternity in a toy store must seem like heaven to the spirit of this little boy, right?

McALLEN RESTAURANTS

DELIA'S
3400 North 10th Street
McAllen 78501
(956) 627-2532

If you ask anyone in McAllen where to get the best tamales in town (or in Texas, or in the world, depending on whom you ask), this place is it. They're open for breakfast, lunch, and dinner, or you can call for takeout.

RUDY'S COUNTRY STORE AND BAR-B-Q
209 West Nolana Loop
Pharr 78577
(956) 781-8888
www.rudysbbq.com

Rudy's is a regional chain—and a good one. It's essentially a meat market that sells meat cooked over pits fueled with oak rather than the faster-burning mesquite that most barbecue joints use. Meat cooks in a dry spice rather than a sauce, although Rudy's provides its proprietary brand of sauce and sells it throughout the nation.

Rudy's restaurants have a country store look to them, with lots of wood, red paint, an awning over the entrance, and an ice machine out front. Meat is sold by the pound. Try the jalapeño sausage, lean brisket, and pork spareribs. They have the usual sides (coleslaw, beans, potato salad), along with creamed corn and jumbo smoked potatoes.

Your best bet for dessert: banana pudding or cobbler.

Rudy's is located in Pharr (pronounced "far"), just east of McAllen. Don't worry; it's a short drive. You don't have to travel Pharr.

You have a couple of choices when it comes to searching for ghosts off the beaten path: One route is best taken from Laredo, while the other is best approached from Brownsville or McAllen.

Carrizo Springs, a town of 6,000 residents, lays claim to two haunted buildings. One is the Dimmit County Courthouse, and the other is Dimmit Memorial Hospital.

The **Dimmit County Courthouse** was built in 1884. Although modest by Texas standards, the courthouse stands out among its peers for one reason: It's haunted.

Courthouse workers say that late at night the sound of footsteps can be heard on the stairs leading to the second floor. Some have reported the faint sound of keys rattling. The footsteps are believed to belong to a former sheriff.

In the old days the county sheriff lived in the courthouse. Legend has it that two unknown assailants broke into the courthouse and killed the sheriff. Now his ghost is believed to haunt the place, and his footsteps can be heard ascending the stairs to his second-floor residence.

The second building said to be haunted—the **Dimmit Memorial Hospital**—is home to the spirit of a former nurse. She is sometimes seen at night, between 8:00 p.m. and 2:00 a.m., in the nursery. The nurse stands out because she's wearing an old-fashioned nurse's uniform instead of the scrubs worn by today's nurses. No one seems to know why this nurse haunts the place or why she favors the nursery. Did she work there? Perhaps she just wants to make sure the babies are well cared for.

You can enjoy lunch or dinner at various chain restaurants in Carrizo Springs. Or, for a taste of local fare, try **Mi**

Casa Steakhouse (2209 North First Street, 830-876-3778). Their specialty? Steaks. You'll also get a good meal at **Rosita's Restaurant** (604 North First Street, 830-876-3825). You can't go wrong with the enchiladas, crisp tacos, and Mexican rice and refried beans.

Your second choice for a day trip will take you to the small town of Lasara and the slightly larger town of Port Isabel. **Lasara** is a small town of 1,000 people located 24 miles northwest of Harlingen. The ghost that haunts this area is usually encountered on the road between Raymondville and U.S. Highway 281.

The road is known as Farm-to-Market Road (FM) 186. Travelers through this remote area have reported seeing a man walking on the side of the road. Those brave enough to offer a ride to this hitchhiker say the man appears to be a real human.

He asks for a ride to Lasara Cemetery. He doesn't say much of anything other than that. Witnesses say they feel a sense of sorrow in the man and a coldness that pervades everything around him. Then, as the man gets out of the car, he disappears without a trace.

The other haunted location in this area is the **Port Isabel Lighthouse State Historic Site.**

Port Isabel is a town of 5,000 people located 21 miles northeast of Brownsville. The Port Isabel Lighthouse is a state historic site with a visitor center. The lighthouse was built in 1852 to help sea captains navigate the low-lying Texas coast.

This 72-foot structure is the only original Texas lighthouse open to the public. The ghost you might encounter is said to be the spirit of a young man who died on his seventeenth birthday. His friends dared him to go to the seventeenth step of this lighthouse and remain there for seventeen minutes.

No one knows why they considered this a dare. Had ghostly spirits been spotted there? Was there some sort of plot against the young man? Whatever the reason, after seventeen minutes, his friends went up to get him and found the young man dead from unknown causes. To this day, when you climb the lighthouse stairs, visitors are reminded of this story when they ascend the stairs—because the seventeenth step eerily creaks when stepped upon.

Dia de los Muertos, or Day of the Dead, is celebrated at the end of October in many South Texas towns. This Mexican tradition pays tribute to those who have passed on to the next world. Although it may sound a tad morbid, Day of the Dead is anything but.

In Port Isabel, the day is commemorated with various programs by the Museums of Port Isabel. The **Port Isabel Day of the Dead Celebration** (317 East Railroad Avenue, 956-943-7602, www.portisabelmuseums.com/dod) features exhibits of Day of the Dead altars created by local college students, cemetery tours, lectures, music, dances, poems, and stories—all with a deadly theme. You can learn how to make your own Day of the Dead altars as well as skull-shaped candy.

When darkness falls, enjoy a scary movie projected on the side of the Port Isabel Lighthouse.

For a place to eat in Port Isabel, try **Pirate's Landing Restaurant** (110 North Garcia Street, 956-943-3663, pirateslandingrestaurant.com). Or head to Raymondville, 60 miles northwest of Port Isabel, for a meal at **Boot Company Bar & Grill** (205 East Hidalgo Street, 956-689-3850).

CENTRAL TEXAS

Austin

Austin is the capital of Texas and home to the state capitol building, the governor's mansion, the University of Texas at Austin, a thriving live-music scene, and one of the largest technology sectors in the United States.

The first documented settlement here occurred in 1835. It was originally named Waterloo in 1837, but Mirabeau B. Lamar, who served as the third president of the Republic of Texas, renamed the city in honor of Stephen F. Austin, leader of the first successful U.S. attempt to colonize Texas.

Austin is the fourth-largest city in Texas and the sixteenth largest in the United States. Its population of over 926,000 makes it the economic and cultural core of the Austin–Round Rock (Round Rock is a suburb north of Austin) metropolitan area, with a population of just over two million.

Austin is also the coolest city in Texas. Not as in cool temperatures—as in a cool city to visit and live in. The city long ago dubbed itself "The Live Music Capital of the World." Its downtown has a thriving entertainment district, and the city is packed with great restaurants, diverse shops, and health-conscious residents who can be seen walking, biking, and jogging along the popular hike-and-bike trail along Town Lake (a section of the Colorado River).

Austin's ghosts seem to enjoy the downtown area as much as anyone. You'll find them haunting popular bars such as The Tavern, restaurants like the Austin Pizza Garden, hotels, and even a photography studio. The area near the university also seems to be popular among the paranormal, with ghosts haunting a couple of bed-and-breakfasts in an old Austin neighborhood.

Spectral visitors in this city include those of a four-year-old daughter of a U.S. senator, a "possessed" remote-controlled car, and the spirit of a prostitute named Emily, who was killed in a bar fight.

AUSTIN ACCOMMODATIONS

Austin's Inn at Pearl Street

809 West Martin Luther King Boulevard
Austin 78701
(512) 478-0051 or (800) 494-2261
www.innpearl.com

Ghosts are believed to haunt both the Victoria House and the Burton House at this four-building B&B near the University of Texas. They first made their presence known when the owner was in the process of renovating both homes. Construction workers reported hearing strange noises and feeling as though they were being watched. One worker refused to stay after nightfall because he believed the house to be haunted.

In her book *Haunted Texas Vacations,* author Lisa Farwell writes that a carpenter reported seeing a female apparition carrying a child from one room to another. He later claimed to have seen her sitting in a rocking chair, rocking a small child. Perhaps it was the ghost of Stella Snider, one of the home's early residents, who, oddly enough, lost two children at the age of two.

The inn's owner, Jill Bickford, told Farwell about an incident that took place during renovations of the Victoria House. She arrived one night and spotted a light in an upstairs window. Although the home was unoccupied at the time, that's not what makes the occurrence so unusual; the fact that the home had not been wired for electricity does. Bickford went around to the back of the house, but by that time the light had disappeared. She was never able to explain the source of this strange light.

This bed-and-breakfast inn is located in a neighborhood known as Judges Hill. It acquired that name in the 1800s when Judge Elijah Sterling Clark Robertson built the first home there. Other judges and attorneys built homes there too, and thus the name.

The inn's ten guest rooms are situated in four buildings. One is the original Greek Revival home, known as the Victoria House. The Burton House next door is also available for stays. The other two buildings are a historic cottage and a modern two-unit studio building constructed for extended stays.

The rooms are beautifully decorated with antiques and knickknacks from around the world. You'll enjoy yourself amid the inn's quiet elegance and comfortable surroundings. Outdoor areas are shaded by stately oaks and splashed with colorful flowers. You're also just a few blocks from one of the largest universities in the world and the shopping area known as "The Drag" that runs along the west side of the campus.

Amenities include private bathrooms, flat-screen TV with cable TV/DVD, Wi-Fi, free local calls, a clock radio, bathrobes for in-house use, hair dryer, toiletries, iron and ironing board, turn-down service, and complimentary Texas wine. Some rooms also come with a Jacuzzi tub, a small refrigerator, and a coffeemaker.

CARRINGTON'S BLUFF BED & BREAKFAST
1900 David Street
Austin 78705
(830) 995-2220
www.carringtonhousebb.com

The two spirits who reside at this 1877 English country house don't have names. Apparitions have been reported, but no one has been able to give a good description other than having a feeling that one is male and the other female. A female ghost is believed to haunt the main house, while a male spirit resides in the cottage.

Guests and staff members say both ghosts seem friendly. They report the feeling of being watched, and footsteps often are heard coming from empty parts of the house. Guests have reported finding things in their rooms moved, while the housekeeping staff recounts times when rooms they have just cleaned become messy a few minutes later for no apparent reason.

In their book *A Texas Guide to Haunted Restaurants, Taverns, and Inns,* authors Robert Wlodarski and Anne Powell Wlodarski report two incidents believed to be related to paranormal activity. One involved the innkeepers, who were living in the cottage at the time. For fourteen straight nights, their television turned on exactly at midnight despite the fact that the only way to turn it on was by pulling a knob on the television.

The unusual activity stopped and then resumed a month later, only this time the television came on at 3:00 a.m.—for seven consecutive days. The innkeepers finally told the ghosts they could do whatever they wanted during the day, but to please let them sleep at night. The television never turned on by itself again.

A second incident involved a guest who was shampooing his hair in the shower. He had closed his eyes to keep shampoo from getting in them when he felt someone massaging his scalp. At first, the man thought his wife had joined him in the shower, until he remembered that he had locked the bathroom door.

If the thought of sharing a shower with a ghost disturbs you, consider wearing a bathing suit. Who knows, you might end up running for your life, and you wouldn't want to offend the other guests.

This house traces its roots to the days of the Republic of Texas, when a shopkeeper named L. D. Carrington purchased what was once a twenty-two-acre site. Located in central Austin not far from the University of Texas, this B&B offers a great combination of comfort, seclusion, amenities, and access to everything Austin has to offer.

Carrington's Bluff has both a main house and a "Writer's Cottage" (built in 1920) across the street. Together, the two homes offer hardwood floors, high ceilings, and eight guest rooms decorated with antiques and set amid an acre of trees on a bluff overlooking a popular Austin park. The main house features a 35-foot-long porch, where you can relax and enjoy a free beverage from the kitchen.

Business services include fax, dry cleaning, delivery or mail services, and free wireless Internet access. Room amenities include cable TV, bathrobes, hair dryers, Matrix hair care products, irons and ironing boards, free local phone calls, in-room coffee and tea service, and a video library.

This cozy inn also offers spa services such as massages, manicures, and pedicures. Breakfast is served daily in the dining room, featuring homemade granola, breakfast meats, fresh fruit, and gourmet coffee. The proprietors here have a fondness for Bluebell ice cream. Bluebell is a Texas brand made in a small town east of Austin. Several varieties are available for dessert or a snack.

THE DRISKILL HOTEL
604 Brazos Street
Austin 78701
(512) 474-5911 or (800) 252-9367
www.driskillhotel.com

The Driskill Hotel is a Texas landmark constructed in 1886 by cattle baron Jesse Lincoln Driskill. Through the years, it has become one of the most haunted sites in Texas. The Driskill's staff counts several ghosts among its regulars. One is Colonel Driskill himself. Driskill is said to smoke cigars (the smell has been reported by guests and employees) and turn bathroom lights on and off.

Another spirit is the four-year-old daughter of a U.S. senator, who died from a tumble down the hotel's grand staircase. Employees have reported hearing a child's laughter and the sound of someone bouncing a ball.

Yet another ghost is a former longtime resident, whose spirit can sometimes be seen on the fifth floor near the elevators looking at a pocket watch. His name was Peter J. Lawless. He lived in the hotel from 1886 to 1916, staying on even at times when the hotel closed down. A female ghost known only as Mrs. Bridges also haunts the Driskill. The former Driskill employee, who worked at the front desk, is often spotted walking from the vault into the middle of the lobby where the front desk once stood. She's identifiable by the Victorian dress she wears.

Two brides who committed suicide at the Driskill are also believed to haunt this historic hangout. One hanged herself in her hotel room after her fiancé broke their engagement the night before their wedding. The second woman is said to have been a Houston socialite who fled to the Driskill after her fiancé canceled their wedding plans. She booked a one-week stay at the hotel and went shopping with her former lover's credit cards. Toward the end of the week, she killed herself in her room. A hotel employee found her lying in the bathtub. She had shot herself through a pillow used to muffle the sound.

The first bride can be spotted on the fourth floor in her wedding dress. She paces the hallways, usually when someone is celebrating a wedding or a bachelorette party. The second bride is often seen in the hallways—especially around Halloween—wearing a wedding gown and carrying a gun.

People who work in the hotel and guests who have stayed there say they've felt some invisible presence touching their face and arms, while some guests have reported seeing figures in windows and seated in chairs.

Climb to the third floor and find the painting of a little girl holding flowers. People who have done so report feeling as though something were lifting their heels off the floor. They also report a tingling sensation that left them feeling strange for the next several hours.

Driskill, a Tennessee native and honorary Confederate colonel who moved to Texas in 1849, decided to build a luxurious hotel that would rival those found in New York, Chicago, and San Francisco. Built at a total cost of $400,000, the Driskill hosted the inaugural ball for newly elected Texas governor Sul Ross. Through the years, several other governors have held their inaugural balls at the Driskill. The governor's mansion and the state capitol building are both within walking distance.

Each guest room comes with plush terry robes, European bath amenities, and cotton bed and bath linens. Guest rooms are equipped with three telephones, high-speed Internet access, a minibar, in-room movies, cable TV, and alarm clock radios. Other amenities include a complimentary shoe shine, nightly turndown service, a business center, twice-daily housekeeping, and a twenty-four-hour fitness center.

The Driskill features two places to eat. One is the Driskill Grill, a full-scale restaurant with traditional, regional, and "innovative" cuisine created by the restaurant's chefs. The second eatery, known simply as 1886, offers an array of pastries and desserts.

OMNI AUSTIN HOTEL DOWNTOWN
700 San Jacinto Boulevard
Austin 78701
(512) 476-3700
www.omnihotels.com

The ghost that haunts this hotel is believed to be that of a man named Jack who committed suicide by jumping from his balcony. Not much is known about Jack, other than he died without paying his hotel bill. Members of the night staff have heard him moving around in the room that he occupied when he stayed there. Guests have reported noises at night coming from the supposedly empty room where Jack stayed.

The Omni is a top-rated hotel in downtown Austin located eight blocks from the state capitol and within walking distance of many restaurants, nightclubs, stores, and the city's popular hike-and-bike trail that winds along the banks of the Colorado River.

This luxurious hotel features 292 guest rooms, 46 club rooms, 19 one-bedroom suites, and 18 two-bedroom suites. Each comes with a view of the city or the hotel's atrium, along with a fully stocked refreshment center, coffeemaker, plush robes, hair dryer, iron and ironing board, evening turndown service, newspaper, and alarm clock. You'll also find complimentary Wi-Fi, two dual-line telephones with dataports, individual climate control, voice mail, on-demand movies, and large flat-screen HDTVs with cable TV. The hotel also offers a heated rooftop swimming pool, fitness center, dry sauna, whirlpool, and spa services. The amenities don't end there. The Omni features a gift shop, post/parcel service, front desk safe deposit boxes, translation services, on-site specialty shops, travel services, and a rental car agency.

Enjoy a cup of coffee or tea and pastries in Morsel's, or partake in cocktails and regional foods in the Atrium Lounge. Ancho's, located in the hotel's glass atrium, specializes in Southwestern cuisine such as flautas, sopes (fried cornmeal cakes topped with meat and vegetables), and braised shredded duck topped with cucumber habañero sauce.

SUPER 8 MOTEL
1201 North I-35, I-35 and 12th Street
Austin 78702
(512) 472-8331
www.super8.com

This downtown motel, newly remodeled in 2016, is convenient to most of the city's haunted sites. It's also within walking distance of the entertainment district, state capitol building, and the hike-and-bike trail along Town Lake. It's included here for the budget-conscious traveler who wants to be near the haunted action.

Amenities at this sixty-room, two-story hotel include a swimming pool, outdoor barbecue area, laundry facilities, free parking, patio, complimentary breakfast, and both a television and free coffee in the lobby. Rooms come with free Wi-Fi, cable/satellite TV with premium channels, refrigerator, housekeeping service, air conditioning, voice mail, microwave, and an iron and ironing board.

Although the Super 8 does not have an on-site restaurant, it's within walking distance of several restaurants, including Denny's, Wendy's, P. F. Chang's, Serranos Cafe and Cantina (Mexican), and the Clay Pit (Indian).

AUSTIN ATTRACTIONS
BOB BULLOCK TEXAS STATE HISTORY MUSEUM
1800 North Congress Avenue
Austin 78701
(866) 369-7108
www.thestoryoftexas.com

Named for a powerful former lieutenant governor, the Bob Bullock Museum tells the story of Texas with three floors of exhibits, special effects shows, and an IMAX theater. This three-story building across the street from the University of Texas also houses a restaurant with indoor and outdoor seating and a gift shop.

The museum is north of the haunted capitol building and other downtown haunts. A 35-foot-tall bronze Lone Star sculpture greets visitors in the museum's rotunda, which features a colorful terrazzo floor depicting a campfire scene with themes from the state's past. You can spend an entire day here, if you like, or break it up into several visits. Tickets to the exhibits, special effects shows, and IMAX theater can be purchased separately.

CONGRESS AVENUE BRIDGE BATS
Congress Avenue and First Street in Austin

You won't find ghosts under the Congress Avenue Bridge. You will find, however, find 1.5 million bats. Each night at dusk between March and October, these nocturnal flying mammals come streaming out from beneath the bridge, a veritable river of bats that fly along the south bank of the Colorado River before dispersing into the night.

Bring a lawn chair, a blanket, and something to eat and drink. You'll be joined by a hundred or so other bat watchers who celebrate as these mosquito-eating machines disperse into the night. If you're really crazy about bats, stay all night and watch them return home in the morning.

Come to think of it, you'd better not. You might get arrested for vagrancy.

DAVID GRIMES PHOTOGRAPHY
503 Neches Street
Austin 78701
(512) 478-0089
www.davidgrimes.com

David Grimes is not only a successful Austin photographer, but he's also a friend of the paranormal, as evidenced by his website, which devotes a page to the many ghosts known to inhabit his studio. He seems to enjoy their presence.

The downtown studio is known as "The Hideout." It's named after a clearing in a banana grove behind the Houston home where Grimes grew up. To get there, you had to crawl through a kid-size tunnel of vegetation.

Grimes has chronicled several unusual occurrences in his studio, where some of the biggest companies in the state (such as Dell, IBM, and DuPont) have come for his artistic services. The result of one odd occurrence is shown on his website: It's a pint-size glass that Grimes placed on a counter one day while talking on the telephone. To his amazement, the glass split in half—vertically!—as he watched. Grimes didn't know what to make of this. Was it a paranormal event or just one of those odd occurrences in life with no real explanation? Whatever the reason, he decided to keep the glass.

The ghostly events began back when Grimes hired workers to refurbish the old building where the studio now sits. An electrician confronted him one day, asking whether Grimes had gone into the building after they had left and undone some of their work. It seems the electricians would find the wiring they had lain the previous day strewn about the room when they came to work in the morning. Grimes assured them that he would never create more work for men who were charging him by the hour.

That ghost obviously didn't want anyone to see him or her. The "woman in the doorway," in contrast, doesn't mind letting her presence be known, although she'll only allow a peripheral view. She appears in the doorway to the "shoot room." Turn to look at her, however, and she disappears. Visiting canines bark, whine, and dig at the concrete floor where she has been spotted.

One of the most intriguing paranormal events involves a remote-controlled car that became "possessed." Grimes purchased the car for fun because the studio's concrete floors were perfect for racing. It started one morning when Grimes arrived at work and found the car careening around the studio. Thinking the remote control had gone haywire, he removed the batteries. The car continued to run.

Eventually, the car became a regular presence in the studio. It would come up to people, stop, and go around them. Visitors greeted it like they would a friendly dog. One day it stopped without explanation. "I felt like I'd lost a friend," Grimes says.

GOVERNOR'S MANSION
1010 Colorado Street
Austin 78701
(512) 463-5518
www.txfgm.org

Two specters are known to haunt this historic residence. One is none other than Sam Houston, the third governor of

Texas. Houston was forced to abandon the governorship after he refused to support the Confederacy. His ghost has been spotted in the Houston Bedroom, standing in one corner and watching. Houston is hard to miss. The balding, barrel-chested Texan stood well over 6 feet tall.

The other ghost is that of the nineteen-year-old nephew of Governor Pendleton Murrah, who shot himself in the head after a young girl refused his marriage proposal. He was found shortly after midnight sprawled out on his bed. In her book *Haunted Texas Vacations,* Lisa Farwell writes that servants at that time refused to enter the room because they believed it to be haunted by the boy's ghost.

To this day, doors open and footsteps resonate throughout the building. Residents also report cold spots. They say you can also hear quiet sobbing, supposedly from the young man, on quiet days when the mansion is mostly empty.

The governor's mansion, located across the street from the state capitol building, is the oldest continuously occupied executive residence west of the Mississippi. This National Historic Landmark was designed by Austin master builder Abner Cook, who is known for having adapted the Greek Revival style of architecture to the frontier.

The Texas Legislature appropriated $14,500 to build the home. It was finished in 1856, six months after its scheduled completion date. Because he was late in completing the project, Cook had to pay for the governor and his family to stay in a boardinghouse until construction was finished.

The most notable feature of this two-story home are the 29-foot-tall Ionic columns along the front, spanning 16-foot-tall ceilings on the first floor and 13-foot-tall ceilings on the second. The house features a deep veranda, floor-length windows, and wide hallways that provided cooling ventilation in the summer.

Built on a square, the home features four main rooms on each floor divided by a broad central hall. A rear wing held a kitchen and servant's quarters.

NEILL-COCHRAN HOUSE MUSEUM
2310 San Gabriel Street
Austin 78705
(512) 478-2335
www.neill-cochranmuseum.org

The most notable ghost at this museum is Colonel Andrew Neill. Neighbors have reported seeing the colonel riding a white horse around the tree-shrouded grounds, sitting on his balcony at night, and—at times when the colonel must have been feeling bold—sitting on the front porch. Other ghostly events include the sound of footsteps that cannot be explained by a human presence.

Built in 1855, this Greek Revival home is one of Austin's oldest landmarks. It's located a few blocks from the University of Texas at Austin. The state capitol building, Texas governor's mansion, and downtown Austin are all within a dozen or so blocks from the museum and each other.

You'll find antiques dating from 1700 to 1900 in period rooms that include colonial, empire, rococo revival, and Victorian. The home was designed and built by Abner Cook, the architect responsible for most of Austin's elegant historic homes, including the Texas governor's mansion.

The museum is open from 1:00 to 5:00 p.m. Tuesday through Saturday. Self-guided tours can be taken any time during operating hours; guided tours start on the hour. Admission ranges from $4 to $10, depending on age and type of tour; no admission is charged for children under twelve.

Paramount Theatre for the Performing Arts
713 Congress Avenue
Austin 78701
(512) 472-5470
www.austintheatre.org

Despite all the well-known acts that have appeared here, the ghosts believed to haunt this theater don't have a name. Big bands, famous singers, and performers of all stripes have performed here, including legendary magician Harry Houdini.

In her book *Haunted Texas Vacations,* Lisa Farwell writes that actors and employees have reported seeing strange lights in the projection room. They also have felt a presence behind them on the stairs and have witnessed props moving on their own. Farwell recounts a time when a stagehand tried to sleep on a couch near the stage one night. He awoke feeling as though someone were holding him down. He then felt a cold breeze and a passing electrical charge, and the feeling ended.

Perhaps the ghost didn't like the play.

The Paramount Theatre began life in 1915 under the name Majestic Theatre. It's located just a few blocks from the state capitol building on downtown's major thoroughfare. This north/south avenue starts at the capitol and extends south for several miles.

The Paramount Theatre continues to host a wide variety of acts.

Scream Hollow
149 Split Rail Lane
Smithville 78957
www.screamhollow.com

Just 35 miles east of Austin, Scream Hollow puts on its annual Wicked Halloween Park from mid-September through the first week of November each year. The twenty-acre site includes three haunted houses, each with its own theme: Mansion of Terror: Phantoms, once voted the "Number One Haunted House in the Nation" by Lions Gate Films; The Zombie City Factory; and Slaughter Circus. Scream Hollow was featured in *Haunt World* magazine as one of "America's Best Haunted Attractions."

To calm your nerves after a run through the haunted houses, you can visit the on-site Rabid Bat Vampire Bar for music and another type of spirits. A disclaimer on the website recommends parents of children under the age of twelve skip the scarier venues and head straight to the Cackling Witch Café and Bakery for more age-appropriate fare of trendy chicken and waffles or a bacon-and-maple pumpkin muffin. Admission ranges from the "I'm Too Scared" $5 ticket for anyone who wishes to enter the park but keep their blood pressure stable to the $25 "Give Me All You Got" ticket for admission to all three haunted houses; kids ages ten and under get in free with a paying adult.

STATE CAPITOL BUILDING
112 East Eleventh Street
Austin 78701
(512) 305-8400
www.tspb.state.tx.us/CVC/home/home

The website (www.paratexas.com) operated by the Paranormal Investigators of Texas, reports that the ghost of state comptroller Robert M. Love haunts the largest capitol building in the United States. In 1903, while he was sitting at his desk, Love was shot to death by a deranged former employee. Ever since, visitors, staff, and security guards have reported seeing a man dressed in clothes worn during Love's time walking through the halls and through walls or staring out windows.

Investigations by Paranormal Investigators of Texas have turned up "electronic voice phenomena" (EVP); that is, voice recordings that say: "Senator, let's run him," "Thank you, Frank," and "Half-breed." As if that's not enough, this group's website also includes a photo of a "ghost squirrel." OK, so it's probably just an albino squirrel that lives on the grounds. But who knows: It could be the ghost of Rocky, the Flying Squirrel, seeking his long-lost friend, Bullwinkle Moose.

Tales of ghosts go back as far as the days of the Old West. Legend has it that a Texas scout and a native girl hooked up one night in the area where the state capitol building now sits only to be discovered by the girl's father, who killed the scout in a fit of rage. Unable to bear the thought of life without her lover, the girl, Juliet, plunged a knife into her heart. For many years afterward, people reported seeing their ghosts on the capitol grounds, and some say you can still spot them after the sun goes down and the downtown area grows quiet.

In her book *Haunted Texas Vacations*, Lisa Farwell writes that many believe the ghost of a man who worked as a horse trainer for the daughter of a former lieutenant governor haunts the building. Mathew Hansen died in a 1983 fire while staying in the lieutenant governor's capitol apartment. He tried to escape from a window that had been sealed shut and died from smoke inhalation before he could make his escape. After the apartment was restored, cleaning crews reported finding fingerprints on the window even after they had just cleaned it.

The Texas State Capitol is based on the U.S. Capitol building in Washington, D.C. Architect E. E. Myers, who also designed the Colorado and Michigan capitol buildings, was paid $1,700 for his

The New Pledge

The young pledge had long dreamed of joining the fraternity his father and grandfather had belonged to. Male family members had, in fact, belonged to this elite organization at the University of Texas at Austin for five generations.

He had grown up on stories about the wild pranks fraternity brothers pulled on new pledges. He therefore expected to be insulted, embarrassed, and run ragged—all in good fun—before he would be allowed to join.

Pledges were at the mercy of fraternity members. They did what they were told or risked rejection. One popular way to abuse the pledges was to parade them around the fraternity house backyard as though they were a marching band. Most pretended to play musical instruments, while some beat on trash cans for drums.

They were forced to march around the yard while fraternity members threw eggs at them from a second-floor balcony overlooking the backyard. It always ended the same way, with the band forced to march headlong into the deep end of the swimming pool.

The young pledge feared this more than anything, for he had never learned to swim. But he was too embarrassed to tell anyone and survived by grabbing onto the side of the pool.

One day, someone noticed him breaking formation, so it was decided that a special punishment should be meted out. Although he explained that he had never learned to swim, it was decided he would be forced to march alone after the other pledges had gone inside. After an hour, most of the fraternity brothers grew tired of the game. One mean-spirited member stayed behind, however, and decided the punishment wasn't severe enough.

(continued)

So he forced the pledge to strap on a garbage can, but this time the pledge was ordered to turn the drum right side up. He was then ordered to march into the deep end of the pool, where the garbage can quickly filled with water. The idea was to send the pledge to the bottom of the pool, where he would literally be forced to sink or swim.

The fraternity brother laughed as the pledge sank. Two minutes later, when the pledge still hadn't surfaced, he ran to the pool and found the pledge at the bottom. He pulled the pledge from the water and began administering CPR. It didn't work. Now in a panic, the fraternity member decided to hide the body, which he did by pushing it down a heavily forested hill behind the fraternity house.

Two days later, when someone finally noticed him missing, the police were called. His body was discovered three days later when buzzards were spotted circling the hill. An autopsy showed the boy had drowned, which meant someone had removed his body from the pool and pushed it down the hill.

Everyone in the fraternity knew who had done it, but they stuck together and stonewalled the police. With no evidence and no one willing to talk, no one ever served a day for the young pledge's death.

To this day, fraternity members report strange occurrences at this two-story mansion. They feel the presence of some unseen force, as if they're being watched. They also say that, late at night, when everyone is in bed, the sound of drumming can be heard coming from the backyard.

When they look outside toward the pool, they can't help but notice that the surface of the water has been disturbed, as though someone—or something—has either jumped into the pool or climbed out.

design. The building's pink granite cornerstone, which weighs six tons, was laid on March 2, 1885, twenty-five years after Texas declared its independence from Mexico. It took 15,000 rail cars filled with Texas pink granite to build what at the time was the seventh-largest building in the world.

The rotunda's marble floor depicts a Lone Star (the symbol of Texas) surrounded by symbols of the five countries that have ruled the state: France, Spain, Mexico, the Republic of Texas, and the United States. The capitol was severely damaged by fire in 1983 and underwent a major renovation in 1990.

AUSTIN RESTAURANTS
AUSTIN PIZZA GARDEN
6266 Highway 290 West
Austin 78735
(512) 891-9980
www.apgatx.com

Longtime employees and patrons have reported seeing faces on the restaurant's walls. No one seems to know who these faces belong to, and no one has reported hearing any sounds or seeing apparitions. Just the faces. Are these the hallucinations of intoxicated, pizza-stuffed patrons, or does this long, stone building hold secrets from its years prior to becoming a pizza parlor? Most of these faces appear to be male, although their gray, hazy appearance makes it difficult to tell.

This is one of those places with a menu so involved and complicated that you have to study it for fifteen minutes before you can figure it all out. You have a variety of options when it comes to toppings (traditional and "gourmet") and sauces (tomato sauce, walnut pesto, barbecue, or white). The walnut pesto, made from basil, garlic, and walnuts, is fantastic.

Austin Pizza Garden offers both thin and thick crust, as well as white and whole wheat. Spend several minutes designing your own pizza, or play it safe and order one of the Pizza Garden's signature pizzas, such as the Bayou Chicken made with Cajun-spiced chicken, roasted red peppers, red onions, and garlic. Sandwiches and appetizers are available too.

Iron Cactus Mexican Grill & Margarita Bar
606 Trinity Street, Austin 78701, (512) 472-9240 (downtown)
10001 Stonelake Boulevard, Austin 78759, (512) 794-8778
(North Austin)
www.ironcactus.com/dt_austin.asp

The Iron Cactus serves Southwestern cuisine, margaritas, tequilas, and an array of wines and beers. Try the Shiner Bock, a dark beer brewed near Austin. Both locations offer indoor and outdoor dining options.

The food here is a combination of Mexican, Texas, and Southwestern favorites and flavors. Try the jalapeño chicken-fried rib eye, a lightly dusted and battered center-cut rib eye with jalapeño cream gray on Navajo mashed potatoes with roasted vegetables. Or enjoy the Shiner chile relleno made with Shiner Beer–battered poblano pepper stuffed with chicken and cheese and served on a bed of tomatillo and Colorado sauces. The downtown Iron Cactus is near all the central haunted sites, such as the state capitol and the governor's mansion.

The Tavern
922 West Twelfth Street
Austin 78703
(512) 320-8377
www.tavernaustin.com

The ghost that resides at this former bordello is a prostitute named Emily—and perhaps her young daughter—who are believed to have been murdered in the 1940s when a fight broke out among the customers.

Emily has been spotted through an upstairs window at night after closing. Employees have blamed her for breaking dishes and glasses (what a convenient scapegoat!), and she loves changing channels on the TVs.

The building that now houses The Tavern dates back to 1916, when owner R. Niles Graham hired Hugo Kuehne to build a grocery store on Ruiz Street, which in those days lay on the outskirts of Austin. Kuehne, who brought the building plans from Europe, modeled the house after a German public house.

The Enfield Grocery Store operated in the building until moving next door in 1929 so that a steak house could be opened. You could buy the best steaks in town for 50 cents. Legend has it that men could purchase two other popular commodities upstairs in the speakeasy and brothel.

The Tavern came into existence in 1933 following the repeal of Prohibition. It served as a restaurant and bar for everyone from college students to U.S. presidents. The Tavern almost became extinct in 2002 when it no longer met city code, and there was talk of tearing it down.

That's when three longtime Austinites stepped forward to save it. Today it serves as a popular sports bar boasting fifty-two televisions. It's open for lunch, dinner, and late-night snacks. The menu consists of local, regional, and American foods like burgers, steaks, sandwiches, nachos, and the popular chicken-fried steak.

AUSTIN ORGANIZED TOURS AND PARANORMAL GROUPS

AUSTIN GHOST TOURS

617 Congress Avenue
Austin 78701
(512) 853-9826
www.austinghosttours.com

This company boasts that it has been voted as one of the top ten ghost tours in the country. Each Friday and Saturday night, ninety-minute walking tours take people to places like the governor's mansion, haunted downtown businesses, and spots where a serial killer who hunted the streets in 1885 left his victims. Tours leave from the downtown Omni Hotel and the Moonshine Patio Bar and Grill.

THE AUSTIN GHOST HUNTERS MEET-UP GROUP

www.meetup.com/Austin-Ghost-Hunters/

This group is open to anyone interested in the paranormal. They meet on the second Monday of each month at haunted— and supposedly haunted—sites throughout the Austin area. Everyone who is interested is given the opportunity to investigate a haunted location. Founded in 2003, this group claims over 550 members.

New Braunfels

New Braunfels (German for "brown rock") is situated 30 miles northeast of San Antonio and 45 miles southwest of Austin. It has a population of nearly 58,000, including a large German American community, whose heritage is celebrated each November at Wurstfest (German for "sausage festival").

German nobleman Prince Carl of Solms-Braunfels established the town in 1845, naming it for the city of Braunfels, his hometown in Germany. Prince Carl was commissioner general of the Society for the Protection of German Immigrants in Texas, an organization that recruited hundreds of people in Germany to settle in the state. Immigrants began arriving from Germany in December 1844 and by 1845 began settling in the New Braunfels area. Soon after founding the city, Prince Carl returned to Germany and never set foot in Texas again.

Today, New Braunfels is home to a still-thriving German culture and one of the most popular water parks in the nation. Schlitterbahn draws thousands of visitors each summer, as do the Guadalupe and Comal Rivers, which attract revelers who float downstream on inner tubes.

This quaint city with two rivers running through it is home to the Gruene Historical District, consisting of restaurants, shops, and bed-and-breakfast inns. Landa Park offers a beautiful escape for those who want to relax or play.

NEW BRAUNFELS ACCOMMODATIONS
Faust Hotel & Brewing Co.

240 South Seguin Avenue
New Braunfels 78130
(830) 625-7791
www.fausthotel.com

The most noteworthy ghost to haunt this historic hotel is the hotel's namesake, a New Braunfels businessman named Walter Faust Sr., who has been spotted roaming the halls dressed in a finely tailored suit and wearing the metal-framed glasses for which he was known.

Guests often spot what they describe as a "quaint and old-fashioned man." One former employee who often worked evenings reported that each night at exactly the same time, the elevator doors would open to reveal an empty elevator. He also reported doors opening and closing by themselves and chairs being pushed back into place.

In an article on the realtraveladventures.com website, Rick Moran writes that Faust is credited—or blamed—for rearranging the furniture on the fourth floor and resetting fans in the hallways to "high." One employee reported seeing Faust's portrait illuminated despite the fact that a thunderstorm had cut electricity to the hotel. A hotel maid spotted a little girl walking through a solid wall, and guests and employees have seen a man in early twentieth-century garb getting on the elevator.

Faust opened the then-world-class hotel in 1929 under the name of The Traveler's Hotel. The art nouveau Spanish Renaissance–style hotel, located near rail lines that converged nearby, became the primary meeting place for business travelers from around the nation. The Traveler's Hotel became the Faust Hotel in 1936. It survived the Great Depression and other economic downturns until 1975, when it closed its doors.

Two years later a company called Jackson-Houser and Associates purchased the property and renovated it. They later sold it to new owners, who in 1980 enclosed the small courtyard to create a lounge. Another owner purchased the hotel in 1982, and a more extensive renovation began. The four-story brick hotel became a Texas Historic Landmark in 1985 and later joined the National Register of Historic Places. Located in downtown New Braunfels, the Faust includes a microbrewery, a gourmet dining room, and 1930s-era antiques. Amenities include free breakfast, parking, wireless Internet access, and coffee in the lobby. The hotel features fifty-nine rooms and two suites.

The lobby is decorated in dark shades of brown and burgundy. A grand piano, handcrafted furnishings, and 1930s artwork give the lobby a unique look and feel. Color schemes grow lighter in tone as the floors ascend. Coordinating carpet, drapes, and bedspreads complement the color schemes and the antique furnishings.

PRINCE SOLMS INN BED & BREAKFAST
295 East San Antonio Street
New Braunfels 78130
(830) 625-9169 or (800) 625-9169
www.princesolmsinn.com

The ghost that haunts the Prince Solms Inn is believed to be a young woman whose wedding day turned into the worst day of her life. In the early part of the twentieth century, the young woman and her family came to the Comal Hotel (later renamed the Prince Solms Inn) to celebrate her wedding.

On her wedding day, the woman waited and waited for her future husband to arrive but to no avail. Seeing their distraught sister, her two brothers set out to find the man who had jilted her with plans to bring him back to do his duty.

147

They followed his tracks from town to town until the tracks gave out. The brothers returned to their sister to report that they feared something awful had happened to her husband-to-be. The woman refused to believe it and insisted on staying in the hotel until he arrived. The hotel management eventually gave her a job, and she later became the innkeeper. She waited more than twenty years for her lover to arrive, but died in the early 1930s.

Then, in 1935 a young man strode through the front doors and headed toward the staircase. The new innkeeper approached the man, who ignored her and proceeded up the stairs. The innkeeper looked up and to her amazement saw a young woman dressed in a wedding gown standing at the top of the stairs. They embraced, kissed, and disappeared. The innkeeper recognized the woman as the one who had waited for her lover all those years!

The Prince Solms Inn, one block east of the town plaza, has been in continuous operation since 1898. Now a bed-and-breakfast, the property includes the original Comal Hotel building, a former feed store, and a private home.

The Eggeling family built and operated the hotel for fifty years. Emilie Eggeling, an early New Braunfels settler, hired a German builder named Christian Henry to erect an inn that would endure. Its base is set on 36-inch footings with walls of brick and stone 3 feet thick in the cellar and 18 inches thick on the first and second floors. The exterior is made from soft, beige-colored brick handmade on the banks of the Guadalupe River. The lumber used to build the inn is cypress milled from giant trees cut from the riverbanks.

Ceilings reach 14 feet on the first floor and 13 feet on the second. The entry doors stand 10 feet high and are augmented with detailed etched glass. They came from a Galveston hotel destroyed by the 1900 hurricane that killed 6,000 people. The bronze fittings that hold the doors in place were purchased in Europe.

The Prince Solms Inn offers two luxury suites on the first floor and eight guest rooms on the second, all with private baths. The rooms and parlor are furnished with antiques, beautiful lighting fixtures, paintings, and prints. The stone patio and part of the courtyard were built with stones from the old Comal County Jail.

The former New Braunfels Feed Store, built in 1860, was converted into a guest house with three guest rooms with private baths. Its 11-foot ceilings allow for lofts in two bedrooms, which contain three double beds that are perfect for children. The Joseph Klein House, built by a German settler in 1852, consists of a living room with a queen sleeper sofa, a bedroom with a queen-size bed, and a kitchen.

Amenities include antique furnishings, tall windows, telephones, clock radios, and cable TV. Rooms come with 400-thread-count sheets, thick Turkish towels, central heat and air, and ceiling fans. Guests enjoy fresh-scented oatmeal soaps, rosemary and cedar conditioning shampoos, and rosemary-scented bubble bath. Guests also enjoy bottled water, chocolate chip cookies, and pretzels upon their arrival.

Breakfasts may include homemade muffins, cream cheese eggs, Italian breakfast sausage, thick-sliced smoked bacon, sausage pie, bananas Foster pancakes, sausage kolaches, stuffed French toast, orange juice, fresh fruit, coffee, and an assortment of teas.

An on-site spa and piano bar add to this inn's comforts.

No wonder the spirit of the jilted young bride doesn't want to leave. Her ghost has been seen several times since 1935. According to the inn's website, the woman was most recently seen in the cellar in 1960. She is always dressed in her wedding gown and wears a joyful smile that can only be attributed to the arrival of her long-lost love.

NEW BRAUNFELS ATTRACTIONS

GRUENE HISTORIC DISTRICT
Southern edge of New Braunfels
www.gruenetexas.com

Not far from the haunted Prince Solms Inn you'll find the Gruene Historic District, located within the New Braunfels city limits. The town of Gruene (pronounced "green") was founded in 1872 by a German farmer named Herman D. Gruene.

This former cotton-producing town is now home to restaurants, antiques shops, bed-and-breakfasts, a historic dance hall, and art studios. Almost all are located in historic buildings renovated for their new purpose.

Gruene Hall, built in the 1880s, claims to be the oldest dance hall in Texas. A historic water tower stands behind it, and the former Gruene family home now operates as the Gruene Mansion Inn. You'll find an old-fashioned drugstore here, a wine-tasting studio (savor the Sangiovese, a light-bodied, semidry red, and the Texas Hill Country pinot grigio, a semiwhite wine), and nearby businesses that rent tubes for floating down the Guadalupe River.

Gruene Market Days are held the third weekend of every month from February to November. Shop from among the more than one hundred artisans and craftspeople selling jewelry, sculptures, furniture, pottery, spices, and more.

SCHLITTERBAHN WATERPARK RESORT
381 East Austin Street
New Braunfels 78130
(830) 625-2351
www.schlitterbahn.com/nb/

The New Braunfels Schlitterbahn was once named the best water park in the nation by the Travel Channel. In years past, it also has received top awards for the World's Best Waterpark, the World's Best Waterpark Landscaping, and the World's Best Waterpark Ride at the Golden Ticket Awards. The Golden Ticket Awards are the Academy Awards of the amusement park industry. The winners are chosen based on the results of an international survey conducted among hundreds of amusement park aficionados. As recently as 2015 it received a Traveler's Choice award from TripAdvisor.com.

Schlitterbahn has dozens of water attractions spread over seventy acres that provide entertainment for every age and thrill level. Visitors have access to several miles of tubing, seven children's water playgrounds, seventeen waterslides, the world's first surfing machine, and three uphill water coasters. The resort side of this park offers accommodations for those who want to attend more than a single day.

TUBING

New Braunfels
(800) 572-2626
http://innewbraunfels.com/chamber/

New Braunfels may be the tubing capital of the world. It certainly is the tubing capital of Texas. Each summer, thousands of visitors drive from Austin, San Antonio, Houston, and the rest of the state to rent an inner tube and float down the Guadalupe and Comal Rivers.

Tubes are available with bottoms or without. You can also rent a tube with an ice chest so you can bring your favorite beverages along. Tube rental places are scattered throughout the New Braunfels area. Call the New Braunfels Chamber of Commerce at the number above, or visit the website and click on "Business Directory."

NEW BRAUNFELS RESTAURANTS
Adobe Verde
1724 Hunter Road
New Braunfels 78130
(830) 629-0777
www.adobeverde.com

This Tex-Mex restaurant occupies a building in the Gruene Historic District that served as one of the first electric cotton gins. Back in the gin's early days, sometime in the 1920s, a groundskeeper named Frank hanged himself from the rafters. Frank was devastated over the loss of a recently deceased lover and decided to take his life in order to be with her.

Today, Adobe Verde is a popular eatery in this tourist district. The outside of this wooden building with corrugated tin siding is festooned with colorful neon signs, a festive Adobe Verde sign, and a front porch where you can dine and drink.

The inside of Adobe Verde has even more character. The floors, walls, rafters, and beams are all the original wood used to build the cotton gin. You can dine downstairs in the main room or take the long trip up the steps to the balcony level.

Start your meal with some frog dip. No, it doesn't really have frog meat in it, although they say frog tastes just like chicken. (It doesn't!) The frog dip is made with melted cheese mixed with beef and pico de gallo with guacamole on the side. You use tortilla chips to scoop up this delectable combination.

Adobe Verde makes great fajitas, whether they're beef, chicken, shrimp, or veggie. The meat and veggies are flame broiled (except for the shrimp, which is sautéed) and served with grilled onions and peppers, guacamole, pico de gallo, sour cream, rice, charro beans, and homemade flour tortillas.

You'll find a variety of entrees and combination plates here. A good bet is the tacos adobe. This dish consists of two flour tortillas filled with beef or chicken fajita, jack cheese, frijoles, avocado slices, and salsa Quemada and grilled until crispy. It's served with charro beans, rice, lettuce, tomato, and fresh flour tortillas.

For dessert, sink your teeth into the Xango Tango, a light pastry filled with cheesecake and fried golden brown. It's then topped with vanilla ice cream, caramel, cinnamon, and powdered sugar. Another good choice is the buñeulo, made with vanilla ice cream mixed with caramel and topped with pecans and cinnamon. This tasty mixture is served in a fried shell.

According to www.ghosttraveller.com, Frank enjoys clinking glasses together, turning lights on and off, and running around upstairs.

GRISTMILL RIVER RESTAURANT & BAR

1601 Hunter Road
New Braunfels 78130
(830) 625-0684
www.gristmillrestaurant.com

This American-style restaurant in the Gruene Historic District is directly behind Gruene Hall and situated on a hill above the Guadalupe River. Sit inside the former mill or outside amid pecan and cypress trees.

As an appetizer, try the chicken poblano quesadillas made with poblano pesto, Monterey jack cheese, and chicken. Or try the Texas Torpedoes—six deep-fried jalapeños stuffed with cream cheese and served with ranch dressing.

Recommended entrees include the pepper filet, an 8-ounce bacon-wrapped filet mignon grilled and topped with cracked black pepper and lime herb butter on the side. Another interesting entree is the tomatillo chicken made with marinated grilled chicken breast served over homemade spicy bean sauce and topped with tomatillo verde sauce.

Are burgers your thing? Then try something really different by ordering a wurstburger. No, that doesn't mean it's the worst burger you'll ever have. *Wurst* is German for sausage, and this burger is made with a South Texas Polish wedding sausage, mustard, and the restaurant's special barbecue sauce.

The desserts here can be a little on the heavy side. But who cares? You're on vacation! Try the Jack Daniel's pecan à la mode made with traditional pecan pie ingredients, a trace of Jack Daniel's, and tons of chocolate chips. You can get this served with Blue Bell ice cream or without.

New Braunfels Smokehouse Restaurant
146 South State Highway 46
New Braunfels 78130
(830) 625-2416
www.nbsmokehouse.com

The Smokehouse, as it is commonly called, is a New Braunfels landmark serving German food, homemade soup, salads, and desserts and hickory smoked meats that have made it legendary since 1945.

The restaurant began as a place for residents to store their meat. R. K. Dunbar bought six South Texas ice plants in 1943 that would become the New Braunfels Smokehouse. Customers not only could store their meats here, but they could also have them custom smoked by Benno Schuenemann, who used old German family recipes for curing and smoking.

The Dunbars built a tasting room that was so popular it evolved into a restaurant. Its success has led to a mail-order business used by more than 250,000 customers across the country. Restaurant customers can sit inside or in "The Yard," an outdoor seating area popular in cooler months.

The Smokehouse is open for breakfast, lunch, and dinner. Breakfast offers the usual eggs, pancakes, waffles, and, this being the Smokehouse, a wide variety of smoked meats from which to choose. Bacon, sausage, ham, Canadian bacon, and pork chops are available for breakfast, along with hash browns, grits, French toast, and breakfast tacos.

For lunch or dinner, start with the Wunderbar, an assortment of Smokehouse meats and cheeses, or perhaps some German potato soup with "wisps o' beef." The Smokehouse chef salad with smoked ham, turkey, and two kinds of cheese on a bed of crisp lettuce also is good.

Those with a healthy appetite might want to try the "Ribs and More," which comes with baby back ribs, beef brisket, turkey breast, sausage (smoked or bratwurst), pinto beans, German potato salad, and bread.

And for dessert, try the bread pudding and butter sauce, apple dumpling, apple strudel, or German chocolate cake.

CENTRAL TEXAS DAY TRIPS AND GETAWAY WEEKENDS

One of the best places to go for ghost hunting outside those previously mentioned in this chapter is the town of **Waco,** 100 miles north of Austin. Waco is the twenty-third-largest city by population in Texas and home to Baylor University.

It's also the home of the Dr Pepper Museum, which isn't all that exciting unless you're from Texas or in the soft drink business. It is, however, rather quaint. The most direct way to get to Waco is to head north on I-35. You can't miss it.

Haunted destinations here include the main library on the **Baylor University** campus. The library houses some of Elizabeth Barrett Browning's original works, and apparently old Liz likes to visit them from time to time.

She has been spotted roaming the halls at night, a candle guiding her way. Students have spotted the white-gowned poet at one of the top-floor windows peering outside at passersby. A statue of the late Ms. Browning sits outside the building, welcoming visitors who have come to view her works. Although her arms are by her sides on the statue, legend has it that the shadow her figure casts on the library wall behind her looks as though her arms are held high above her head. Is she signaling a touchdown? Or is there a sinister explanation for her upraised arms?

While you're on campus, take a walk over to **Brooks Hall.** It's said that a mysterious phantom resides on the empty fifth floor of the oldest dorm on the oldest college campus in Texas. Listen carefully and you might hear violin music. Residents of this dorm report lights going off for no reason, the sound of someone tap, tap, tapping, and a cold sensation throughout the occupied fourth floor. Peer closely and look for a cloaked figure holding a candle and staring down at you.

For years, rumors of this phantom have led the curious to gather outside this dorm at midnight. Some have reported seeing the light from what appears to be a floating candle going from room to room. It vanishes for a while and then returns elsewhere.

Legend has it that one night during a storm, a group of students went outside to see if the ghost was active that night. Suddenly, they heard the shattering of glass as one of the top-floor windows blew out. The next morning, after the storm had passed and daylight returned, they went back outside and, to their amazement, discovered absolutely no damage to the window.

If you decide to spend the night in Waco, try **The Cotton Palace Bed & Breakfast** (1910 Austin Avenue, 877-632-2312, www.thecottonpalace.com). This home, built in 1910, offers six rooms/suites and a carriage house that can accommodate visitors. Or, if a medium-priced hotel is more your style, visit **Waco Comfort Suites** (2700 LaSalle Boulevard, 254-537-0413, www.wacocomfortsuites.com).

For fun, you can actually visit the aforementioned **Dr Pepper Museum** (300 South Fifth Street, 254-757-1025, www. drpeppermuseum.com). Here you'll learn the history of America's first soft drink (it's older than Coca-Cola), and you can relax and enjoy a Coke, er, Dr Pepper.

For a place to eat, drop into **DiamondBack's** (217 Mary Avenue, 254-757-2871, www.diamondbackswaco.com) for a grilled steak and some peach cobbler.

NORTH TEXAS

Dallas

Dallas, the ninth-largest city in the United States, covers 384 square miles and is home to an estimated 1.2 million people. This mostly flat city ranges in elevation from 450 feet to 750 feet of prairie dotted with native pecan, cottonwood, and oak trees.

The city grew up along the banks of the Trinity River after John Neely Bryan, a lawyer from Tennessee, visited the area in 1839 and decided it would be a good spot for a trading post. Two years later, after closing out his affairs in Tennessee, Bryan returned to Dallas and started his town. The city formally incorporated on February 2, 1856.

Today, Dallas is a global center for telecommunications, banking, transportation, and computer technology. It is the center of the largest inland metropolitan area in the nation without a navigable link to the ocean.

Dallas is also known for the Dallas Cowboys, the *Dallas* TV show, the Neiman Marcus department store chain, and as the site of President John F. Kennedy's assassination on November 22, 1963.

White Rock Lake in northeast Dallas is the site of one of the most popular ghost stories in Texas. Other specters include a drugstore clerk who haunts the store where he was killed, a jilted bride who returns to the scene of her humiliation, and a ghost named "Harold" who has blood flowing from his eyes.

DALLAS ACCOMMODATIONS
CORINTHIAN BED & BREAKFAST
4125 Junius Street
Dallas 75246
(214) 818-0400, (866) 598-9988
www.corinthianbandb.com

The Corinthian Bed & Breakfast, named for the Corinthian columns along its front, is a few miles west of the Dallas Arboretum and Botanical Garden and the haunted DeGolyer Estate. Everette and Nell DeGolyer would appreciate this place. They loved fine homes, as evidenced by the DeGolyer Estate itself.

Although not nearly as large, the Corinthian is just as beautiful. The home is part of the Peak-Suburban Historic District near Swiss Avenue. Garfield Hackler, MD, professor of surgery at the University of Dallas (later known as Baylor Medical College), had the home built in 1905 at a cost of $4,500.

The home later served as a boardinghouse for young women. It became a B&B shortly after the current owners purchased and restored it in 2001. The six suites are decorated with antique furnishings and decor and come with private bathrooms and king-size beds with pillow-top mattresses. Rooms also come with televisions, telephones, hair dryers, greenery and/or fresh flowers, radios, and wireless Internet access.

The word *breakfast* in this inn's name is appropriate. It begins with early morning coffee on the second floor or in the Garden Room next to the kitchen. Breakfast is a leisurely and somewhat extravagant affair, with fresh juice and fruit, warm breads and pastries, and an entree that varies from day to day.

Stoke up on one of these hearty meals as you prepare yourself for a full day of ghost hunting.

HOTEL ADOLPHUS
1321 Commerce Street
Dallas 75202
(214) 742-8200
www.hoteladolphus.com

A jilted bride haunts this luxury hotel. So does a poltergeist who rearranges beer bottles in the bar's display case. Built in 1912 by beer baron Adolphus Busch, the Hotel Adolphus is an upscale hotel that combines Old World charm with modern-day amenities.

The Hotel Adolphus is reportedly a great place to stay unless the sounds of ghosts talking and playing music bother you. People who have stayed here say it definitely is haunted, but they go on to say they'd stay there again the next time they're in Dallas. That's because the hotel is elegant and ornate and the service so good that those who can afford it don't mind a ghost or two.

Employees and visitors alike report hearing unexplainable conversations, the sound of someone walking down the hall, and music from a distant piano or, less commonly, a band playing music from the Big Band era.

The nineteenth floor, which once served as the hotel's ballroom, is the site where most of the otherworldly activity takes place. People report feeling as if they're being watched. They also report being tapped on the shoulder by an invisible presence and hearing a woman crying in the next (unoccupied) room.

An article by Brian Anderson in the October 28, 2003, edition of the *Dallas Morning News* reported two particularly spooky incidents. The first occurred in the weeks following a frequent customer's death. Employees claimed to have repeatedly seen the dead woman sitting at her favorite table near the front of the hotel restaurant.

On another occasion, two women packed their bags and ran when they woke up in the middle of the night to find a strange man standing in their room. At other times, employees have reported windows flinging open for no reason and a blast of cold air rushing in.

The jilted bride is the most commonly spotted ghost at the Hotel Adolphus. The woman is believed to have hanged herself in the 1930s after her fiancé backed out of their marriage at the last minute. Unable to bear a life without him, the woman took her life not far from the spot where she had been scheduled to take her vows. The bride is the one who is believed to awaken guests in the middle of the night with her crying.

The Hotel Adolphus is a "baroque masterpiece" that "ushered in a grand new era of sophisticated Dallas lodging," according to its website. The Adolphus, which opened on October 5, 1912, was built by the founder of the Anheuser-Busch company, who wanted to build the first ritzy hotel in Dallas. He succeeded. Flemish tapestries and a Victorian Steinway once owned by the Guggenheims are among the amenities you'll find at this hotel, which *Travel + Leisure* included among the world's 500 best hotels in 2007. *Travel + Leisure* listed the hotel's "competitive edge" (one of the categories used to rate hotels) as its museum-quality collection of art and antiques, including Louis XV chairs.

Its 422 guest rooms and suites have been restored and furnished with plush beds, Queen Anne furnishings, and specially commissioned fabrics. Pillow-top mattresses, 250-thread-count triple sheets, 32-inch flat-screen TVs with DVD player, cable, and in-room movies are among the amenities found in each room. You'll also find free wireless high-speed Internet access, dataports, cordless dual-line telephones, irons and ironing boards, coffeemakers, gourmet minibars, and large bathrooms with terry robes, hair dryers, and a makeup mirror.

Hotel amenities include a business center, fitness center, gift shop, five-star restaurant, florist, and free transportation within a 3-mile radius.

LA QUINTA INN & SUITES DALLAS DOWNTOWN
302 South Houston Street
Dallas 75202
(214) 761-9090 or (877) 396-0334
www.laquintadallasdowntown.com

Opened in 1925 as the Hotel Lawrence, this recently renovated hotel in the heart of Dallas is within walking distance of the John F. Kennedy Memorial Plaza, the Sixth Floor Museum at Dealey Plaza, and the West End Historic District, as well as just across the street from Dallas Union Station.

According to the website www.theshadowlands.net, a woman who jumped to her death from a tenth-floor suite in the 1940s is said to haunt this historic luxury hotel. The unnamed woman was staying in the presidential suite and climbed over the railing of her balcony; she met her demise when she met the pavement below.

Guests and staff on the tenth floor have heard her crying. They also report hearing voices, as though the woman is in deep conversation with someone. Footsteps echo through the hallway, and unexplained cold spots give people the willies. The clicking of high heels pacing back and forth across the lobby has been heard between midnight and 6:00 a.m.

The spirit of a high-stakes gambler is also said to haunt this hotel. He hangs out on the second level, where an illegal casino once operated. No one is sure why the gambler haunts this place. Perhaps he's hoping for a quick game of blackjack or one more roll of the dice. Or maybe someone still owes him money.

The Hook

The two young lovers from De Soto, a small town south of Dallas, had decided to leave town for a few hours. There was nothing to do in De Soto except hang out at the Dairy Queen or make out at the city park.

The police always disturbed them whenever they went "parking," so they decided to head for a secluded spot at White Rock Lake, in northeast Dallas. Thanks to the interstate, the trip didn't take all that long, so within an hour they were almost there.

They were listening to music on the radio when the deejay interrupted. An inmate at the Dallas Hospital for the Criminally Insane had escaped and was on the loose. The man had been committed, the deejay said, for the bloody murder of a young couple at a lake in North Texas.

The teenagers looked at one another with wide eyes.

"That's creepy," the girl said. "Maybe we should head back."

"What for?" said the boy, trying to act brave. "That hospital is miles from the lake."

They drove on for a while without speaking, the sound of Steely Dan and Journey blasting from the radio. They found the entrance to White Rock Lake and drove inside. Just then, the music stopped again as the deejay returned.

The Associated Press had gotten hold of the story, the deejay said, and had looked into the escaped inmate's past. The man had served in Vietnam, where he lost his right arm at the elbow when a sniper put a bullet through it. Doctors had fitted the man with a prosthetic arm. The man later fitted the arm with a razor-sharp hook, which he had used to kill the young couple.

The hook had been removed when he was arrested and was kept in the prison's property room. The man, it turns out, had broken into the room just before escaping from prison and had taken the hook with him. Furthermore, the deejay said, the man had been spotted in the north Dallas area near White Rock Lake.

"We should go home," the girl whined.

"No way," the young man said. "What are the odds of us running into him? Do you know how big this lake is? Besides, I know a secluded spot where no one will ever find us."

The boy drove to the secluded spot, parked the car, and leaned over to kiss his girlfriend. Caught up in their passion, they at first didn't hear the scratching sound of metal against metal.

"What's that?" the girl suddenly said.

They stopped and listened. An owl hooted in a nearby tree. "It's just an owl," the boy said.

"No, it was something else," the girl protested.

The boy ignored her and resumed his advances. The girl eventually relaxed only to hear the sound again a few minutes later. Each time the girl pushed her boyfriend away and listened, and each time her boyfriend, who had heard nothing, assured her it was nothing. It happened twice more before the girl finally had had enough.

"I'm scared," she said. "Take me home!"

"No!" the boy said. "We just got here."

"Take me home right now," she said, "or I'll walk home!"

(continued)

The girl reached for the door handle when the boy stopped her. "OK, I'll take you home, you little scaredy cat."

They drove home to De Soto and headed straight for the girl's house. The boy stopped the car and looked at her.

"Thanks for ruining a perfectly good night," he said.

"I heard something creepy," she protested.

"It was just your imagination."

"Maybe it was," the girl admitted, "but that place gave me the creeps." The boy leaned in to kiss her again.

"Get away!" she said. "Is that all you think about?"

The boy sighed in exasperation and decided to give up for the night. Ever the gentleman, he got out of the car and walked around to open her door. He stopped when he got there, his eyes wide with horror. For there, hanging from the door handle, was a razor-sharp hook with blood dripping from it!

Today's La Quinta describes itself as a "European-style boutique" hotel. Rooms come with a flat-screen HDTV and cable TV, pillow-top mattresses, coffeemaker, hair dryer, irons and ironing boards, and free Wi-Fi. Hotel amenities include meeting centers, a state-of-the-art fitness room, a complimentary breakfast, and a convenient market stocked with snacks and essentials.

DALLAS ATTRACTIONS

DALLAS CITY HALL
1500 Marilla Street
Dallas 75201
(214) 670-3011
www.dallascityhall.com

A visit to city hall may scare the bejeebers out of some people. The thought of tangling with bureaucratic red tape and standing in interminably long lines is enough to spook anyone. Although this city hall isn't known to be haunted, it's a convenient stop while visiting the Dallas Heritage Village and its haunted Millermore House.

As a tourist, you can enjoy the luxury of visiting city hall merely to appreciate its stunning architecture. Renowned architect I. M. Pei designed this avant-garde building that resembles an inverted pyramid. Built in 1978, it measures 560 feet long and 122 feet (ten stories) high.

DeGolyer Estate
8525 Garland Road
Dallas 75218
(214) 515-6500
www.dallasarboretum.org

The spirits that roam the DeGolyer Estate like to watch people and move items around. No one is sure who the ghosts are. It might be Everette L. DeGolyer, a successful Texas oilman, and his wife, Nell Goodrich DeGolyer, who built and lived in the hacienda-style home.

Visitors, employees, and docents at this historic estate at the Dallas Arboretum and Botanical Garden report the uncomfortable feeling of being watched. Others say they feel as if they're intruding when they walk into a room. The 21,000-square-foot home, built in 1940, is listed on the National Register of Historic Places. It's part of the Dallas Arboretum and can be rented for special occasions.

The DeGolyer Garden Cafe/Loggia in the back of the home overlooks White Rock Lake, which also happens to be haunted. The house has thirteen rooms, seven bathrooms, an attached greenhouse, a four-car garage, and two-bedroom servants' quarters. The home is open for tours.

ECKERD'S DRUGS
8686 Ferguson Road
Dallas 75228
(214) 320-0892

A ghost named Wayne haunts this drugstore. Wayne worked at the store a few years back, unloading delivery trucks and stocking the shelves. He worked nights when the store was closed because that was the best time to restock the shelves.

One morning around sunrise, as Wayne was leaving the store, three men jumped him in an effort to rob him. Wayne had been robbed several times before while leaving work and this time decided to fight back. Unfortunately for Wayne, one of the robbers pulled out a gun and in the ensuing scuffle unloaded several rounds into the drugstore stocker.

Legend has it that three rounds pierced his heart, and the other three slammed into his head. No amount of drugstore pain relievers was going to help Wayne. He died that day, and ever since his ghost has haunted this place.

Employees say Wayne makes his presence felt by toppling boxes, turning radios on and off, and running upstairs. His footsteps can be heard going up the steps, and cold spots give employees the shivers.

LIZARD LOUNGE
2424 Swiss Avenue
Dallas 75204
(214) 826-4768
www.thelizardlounge.com

The ghosts that haunt the Lizard Lounge may be the spirits of deceased actors upset over the building being turned from a dramatic theater into a nightclub for headbangers and booty shakers.

The Lizard Lounge has been entertaining music and dance lovers since 1992. Its success is attributed to its ability to make music fans of all stripes feel as though it's devoted to people just like them.

One night you'll find the place hopping with hip hoppers. The next night it might be electronic dance music drawing a crowd, and the day after that the place will be filled with black-clad Goths. Sometimes the place is so packed, the energy so high, and the club so dense with cigarette smoke and sweat, revelers take refuge on the rooftop deck to cool off and collect their wits.

In a previous life the building served as a theater for locally produced plays. One of the ghosts who haunt the place is a man dressed in black who, from the descriptions, sounds like an upscale Zorro impersonator. The man in black is dressed in a dark suit, black cape, and black hat. He doesn't carry a sword, though. This Zorro-without-a-sword has been spotted hanging out in the area where the audience once sat, although there is nothing in the ghost grapevine describing what this spirit does.

Lisa Farwell, in her book *Haunted Texas Vacations*, tells of an actress named Molly Louise Shepard who performed in the theater in days gone by. One night, Shepard entered her second-floor dressing room and was bombarded with flying glass as the lightbulbs on the vanity exploded for no apparent reason.

Another odd occurrence involved an iron Shepard planned to use to press her costume. She plugged in the iron, turned it to the "cotton" setting, and left the room. A few minutes later, she returned to find the metal face of the iron melted into a puddle. A third instance, Farwell reports, involved a hair dryer that flew through the air, barely missing Shepard's head.

These days, the man in black would fit right in on Goth night at the club. Who knows, that guy you're dancing with to live music might not be "live" himself.

McKinney Avenue Trolley
3153 Oak Grove
Dallas 75204
(214) 855-0006
www.mata.org

This vintage trolley will take you on a tour of downtown Dallas, the arts district, and McKinney Avenue. This isn't one of those buses designed to look like a trolley car. It's an actual electric-powered streetcar that runs on a 3.9-mile loop of track.

The McKinney Avenue Trolley claims to be the largest volunteer-run system in the world. All rides are free. Patrons can climb aboard Rosie (1909), The Green Dragon (1913), Petunio (1920), Matilda (1925), and Winnie (1945), all of which have air-conditioning, an important consideration in the summer. Although the trolley won't take you directly to any haunted destinations, it will take you near enough the downtown haunts to allow you to walk.

Millermore House
1515 South Harwood Street
Dallas 75215
(214) 421-5141
www.dallasheritagevillage.org/supporters/millermore/

A female spirit is said to haunt this 1861 Greek Revival mansion. Employees, volunteers, and visitors have commented on feeling an unseen presence when visiting this historic home in Dallas Heritage Village, a collection of more than thirty restored historic homes that bring the city's history to life.

The female presence is especially felt on the second floor in the area that once held a nursery and master bedroom. Some believe the spirit belongs to Minerva Barnes Miller, the second wife of William Brown Miller, who built the house for her.

His wife died in 1856, six years before the home was completed. A figure dressed in clothes resembling those worn by Minerva has been spotted in an upstairs window, and several people have spotted something moving inside the house somewhere between the nursery and the master bedroom.

No one knows why Minerva might be haunting the place. Perhaps it's because she was never able to enjoy it when she was alive. Maybe her presence in and around the nursery is an indication that one of her children died in infancy. Visit this two-story home with Ionic columns and a second-floor balcony, and you might be lucky enough to get a glimpse into the past.

PLEASANT GROVE CHRISTIAN CHURCH
1324 Pleasant Drive
Dallas 75217
(214) 391-3159
www.pgccdallas.org

It's been said that children haunt this Dallas church. They run past visitors and then disappear. Banging and howling noises have been reported from all over the building. Witnesses report seeing a child's face in an empty hallway and what may be an adult wielding an ax. The children who haunt this church are believed to be benign.

Church members trace the church's history back to 1875. The church was started in a small rural community east of Dallas known as Pleasant Grove. The city eventually engulfed this small town, but the church still stands on its original plot.

Sons of Hermann Hall
3414 Elm Street
Dallas 75226
(214) 747-4422
www.sonsofhermann.com

Only one of the spirits who occupy this historic hall has a name. The hall was built by German immigrants as a gathering place for their people. The caretaker's name was Louie Bernardt. Louie ran a tight ship. One of the things people remember about him is how he would yell at kids to stop playing inside the hall.

Louie is still at it even in death. Patrons of this hall, who are members of the Sons of Hermann Lodge, have reported hearing the sound of a man yelling at children for playing there. Members don't pay much attention to it. They've grown accustomed to strange occurrences here.

The hall, built in 1910, hosts lodge meetings, dances, and live music. It also hosts more than one ghost, it seems. Regulars report hearing footsteps and the sound of furniture being moved upstairs, which might not be that odd if it weren't for the fact that the second floor is empty. Members have checked the second floor after hearing these sounds and always find the room empty. Regulars just ignore the sounds.

Doors open and close by themselves, pictures fall off walls, and voices other than Louie's have been reported. The Wlodarskis report in their book *A Texas Guide to Haunted Restaurants, Taverns, and Inns* that extras on the hit TV show *Walker, Texas Ranger* witnessed a spooky episode one night while having a drink in the downstairs bar.

According to the story, a man in a top hat and a woman in a long dress entered the hall and proceeded through the downstairs corridor. The crew members waited for them to return and, when they didn't, began to search for them. The couple was never found.

In January 2007, the Metroplex Paranormal Investigations group invited the public on a ghost hunt at the hall. Todd Maternowski, who writes for the website www.pegasus.com, joined the hunt. He didn't see any ghosts or hear anything out of the ordinary. He did, however, come back with forty-three photographs showing orbs of various sizes and brightness. These orbs, mind you, were not visible to the naked eye.

Check out the hall's website for upcoming public events.

THRILLVANIA
I-20 and Wilson Road
Terrell 75160
(972) 524-2868
www.thrillvania.com

This nationally acclaimed Halloween extravaganza sets up every October east of Dallas and features haunted attractions, a midway, food and beverages, and a haunted store. The Haunted Verdun Manor, said to be the former home of one Baron Michael Verdun and his wife, Lady Cassandra, who together hosted fiendish masquerades around the turn of the twentieth century, is a rotting mansion with an overgrown cemetery. Cassandra's Labyrinth of Terror takes patrons on a twisted journey filled with vignettes from Lady Cassandra's dangerous and disturbing past. At Dr. Lycan's Trail of Torment, the demented doctor who once assisted the Baron Verdun in his fiendish experiments unleashes his human/monster creations. And Granny Lupus's Séance Theatre, where you can witness ghosts and ghouls and various physical manifestations of the spirits that haunt the Verdun estate, will have you jumping out of your seat.

Turtle Creek Center
2911 Turtle Creek Boulevard
Dallas 75219

"Harold" haunts this high-rise building just north of downtown. He is believed to be the ghost of a successful businessman who worked in the building in the 1980s. According to the website www.shadowlands.net, which is operated by Paranormal Investigations of North Texas (PINS), on September 13, 1989, Harold was found dead one night in his office. No one knows what killed him. It must have been something sinister, because his spirit haunts this place, and he does not look happy.

Witnesses have reported seeing Harold on the stairwell between the thirteenth and fourteenth floors. He has blood seeping from his eyes and wears a terrified look on his face. According to the PINS website, those who have followed him (and no one knows exactly why someone would follow a man who looks like this) say Harold just disappears without warning.

White Rock Lake
Northeast of downtown Dallas
www.whiterocklake.org

The ghost of a young woman clad in either a white dress or a white evening gown haunts this lake in the northeast section of Dallas. Stories about the dripping-wet young woman with long hair go back as far as the 1930s. Although some written accounts report to have merely seen the woman as they're driving through scenic White Rock Lake Park, others have reported giving the woman a ride home.

The story of the "lady in white" goes like this: A young couple is parked at White Rock Lake on a dark night when a young woman dressed in white approaches them. Her hair and white dress are soaked with water. The young woman tells them she fell from a boat and needs to get home.

The young woman sits in the backseat because she doesn't want to get their car wet. They drive the woman to the South Dallas neighborhood where she lives and, when they turn to verify the address, find to their amazement that she is gone. They look for her in and around the car and find nothing, although they do find water on the backseat where the girl had sat.

They decide to go to the address the woman gave them. A man wearing a worried expression answers the door. Yes, he says, he does have a daughter who fits that description. He also informs them that they are the third couple to come to his door with the same story. And then comes the kicker: His daughter had drowned at White Rock Lake three weeks earlier!

DALLAS RESTAURANTS

THE PORCH
2912 North Henderson Avenue
Dallas 75206
(214) 848-2916
www.theporchrestaurant.com

This upscale American gastropub has outdoor seating overlooking Henderson Avenue. It's open seven days a week for lunch, dinner, and weekend brunch. If you're looking for standard pub fare but with a twist, try the Stodg burger, which comes topped with bacon and one egg, sunny side up. For lighter fare, try the blackened redfish or fried (OK, not so light) chicken salad. If you still have room for dessert, the waitstaff highly recommend the Gooey Butter Cake (the description says it all) and the triple chocolate brownie (read: humongous and decadent). If you'd rather stop in for a drink, the inventive cocktails will not disappoint.

RESTAURANT DEGOLYER
8525 Garland Road
Dallas 75218
(214) 515-6512

Restaurant DeGolyer, as you might expect, is located on the grounds of the DeGolyer Estate, which is owned and operated by the Dallas Arboretum and Botanical Garden. In fact, this cafe with outdoor seating is at the back of the house overlooking White Rock Lake, which is said to be haunted by a lady in white.

The spirits of the home's former owners—Everette L. DeGolyer, a prominent Texas oilman, and his wife, Nell Goodrich DeGolyer, are believed to haunt this house and cafe. Those who have been here report an uncomfortable feeling of being watched, while others say they feel like they're intruding when they walk into a room.

You might grow weak ghost hunting at this large estate, so take a break and reenergize with a selection of soups, salads, sandwiches, and desserts. Try the Caesar salad, the Sonoma grilled cheese sandwich, and the pan-seared salmon.

SNUFFER'S BAR AND GRILL
3526 Greeneville Avenue
Dallas 75206
(214) 826-6850
www.snuffers.com

The ghosts at Snuffer's like it when you talk about them. At least, that's how it seems to employees and frequent visitors.

They say that all you have to do to get a ghost to visit is to mention a previous visit. Within a few days after mentioning ghosts, something odd will happen.

Like what, you say? Like cold chills, hearing your voice spoken three times, and feeling a hand on your shoulder. Is that the hand of death trying to get your attention? Ignore him and maybe he'll go away. Keep an eye on your beverage glass. They've been known to move several feet when no one is looking. The ghost or ghosts here don't have a name, and no one knows of any horrible experiences that would explain why the place is haunted.

A man named Pat Snuffer opened the restaurant in 1978. Snuffer says he didn't believe in ghosts until a few months after opening the restaurant. Although they've never done anything to hurt anyone, Snuffer is reluctant to discuss them.

Snuffer's burgers and cheddar fries is what sells most people on the place. Starting as a small, one-room restaurant, Snuffer's has ten locations (and is still growing, according to its website) in Texas. Its menu also has expanded through the years, and now includes salads, turkey and veggie burgers, chicken-fried Black Angus steaks, and sandwiches.

You can't go wrong with the Snuffer's classic burger. It's made with half a pound of freshly ground chuck and served on a grilled poppy seed bun. Each burger is garnished with mustard, pickles, red onions, lettuce, and tomatoes. If you want something different, order a pizza burger with marinara sauce, provolone, and shaved Parmesan.

You really have to try Snuffer's Legendary Cheddar Fries, an item so popular that the name "Snuffer's Legendary Cheddar Fries" is copyrighted. They're made by melting cheddar cheese over, under, and around freshly hand-cut potato fries. Eat them as is or adorn them with bacon, chives, and jalapeños.

Go easy on the jalapeños, though. Those suckers can burn. And remember, if you feel someone place a hand on your shoulder, just keep eating and hope whoever it is goes away.

DALLAS ORGANIZED TOURS AND PARANORMAL GROUPS

METROPLEX PARANORMAL INVESTIGATORS

www.facebook.com/MetroplexParanormalInvestigations

Metroplex Paranormal Investigators is a group of ghost hunters who have investigated more than one hundred sites since the group began in 2001. They use scientific methods to document paranormal activity, with ghost-hunting equipment and two psychics.

Although the psychics and scientists often come to opposing conclusions, they consider this a plus rather than a minus, because they are open-minded and enjoy having fodder for discussions. Their motto is "We Believe You." So if you think you have a ghost, they believe you believe and will do what it takes to document as much paranormal activity as possible.

To join, visit their Facebook page and post a comment.

Denton

Counted among the fastest-growing cities in the United States, Denton is the twenty-fifth-largest city in Texas and the eleventh largest in the Dallas-Fort Worth metroplex. The three cities—Dallas, Fort Worth, and Denton—form an area called the "Golden Triangle of North Texas." Located on the north end of the metropolitan area on I-35, Denton has a population of well over 100,000 and is the county seat of Denton County.

Settled in the mid-1800s and incorporated in 1866, the city is named for John B. Denton, an early pioneer and Texas militia captain. His grave is on the courthouse lawn, and his spirit is rumored to stroll about the grounds from time to time carrying a muzzle-loading rifle, perhaps protecting the town that bears his name. The arrival of a railroad line in 1881 spurred population growth, as did the establishment of two universities—the University of North Texas and Texas Woman's University—within the next twenty years.

In addition to its appeal as a college town, Denton has a vibrant downtown and enough ghosts to warrant a professional ghost tour so that residents and visitors can experience history with a touch of the paranormal. A good many of those ghosts have names. Tour guide Shelly Tucker likes to say that there are so many ghosts because "people come to Denton and never want to leave . . . ever!" She theorizes that spirits linger for a couple of reasons: 1) names of some of the early inhabitants have been lost because fires destroyed county records and those people "just want someone to *remember*," or 2) maybe "they just like the night life in Denton," a city known for its music and storytelling. Two noteworthy festivals take place in the spring: the Denton Arts and Jazz Festival and the Texas Storytelling Festival, which typically starts off with a ghost story concert.

DENTON ACCOMMODATIONS

Closest to downtown haunted sites (within 2 miles) are these chain hotels:

SPRINGHILL SUITES BY MARRIOTT

1434 Centre Place Drive
Denton 76205
(940) 383-4100
www.marriott.com/hotels/travel/dfwsd-springhill-suites-denton

This all-suite hotel boasts a spacious lobby with flexible areas for working, meeting, and relaxing. It is near historic—and sometimes haunted—museums, restaurants, and entertainment venues on or around Denton's famous downtown square. Shoppers can explore the newly renovated Golden Triangle Mall, and the Texas Motor Speedway, home to NASCAR racing, is only twenty minutes away.

Amenities include free Wi-Fi, an indoor pool and fitness center, manager's reception, and a complimentary hot breakfast.

HAMPTON INN & SUITES

1513 Centre Place Drive
Denton 76205
(940) 891-4900
www.hilton.com/search/hp/us/tx/denton

Situated near the heart of downtown and the historic and haunted century-old courthouse, the Hampton Inn & Suites is also within easy reach of Ray Roberts Lake State Park.

Amenities include free coffee and tea in the lobby, free breakfast, high-speed Internet access, fitness facilities, and an outdoor pool.

QUALITY INN & SUITES
1500 Dallas Drive
Denton 76205
(940) 387-3511
www.choicehotels.com/texas/denton/quality-inn-hotels

Less than ten minutes from downtown, the Quality Inn & Suites is only thirty minutes from Dallas/Fort Worth International Airport and forty minutes from Dallas Love Field Airport. North Texas University's Apogee Stadium and the Denton County Historical Museum are nearby.

Amenities include complimentary coffee and weekday newspapers, a free hot breakfast, free Wi-Fi, an outdoor pool, an exercise room, and a business center. Each guest room has a microwave and refrigerator and is pet friendly.

DENTON ATTRACTIONS

AFRICAN AMERICAN MUSEUM IN THE HISTORIC QUAKERTOWN HOUSE
317 West Mulberry Street
Denton 76201
(940) 349-2865
www.dentoncounty.com

A simple frame house located in Denton's Historical Park, within walking distance of the courthouse square, was once part of an African American neighborhood known as Quakertown, named in honor of the abolitionist Quakers who helped slaves traveling the Underground Railroad. The house was built in 1904 but was relocated in the 1920s when the entire Quakertown community was uprooted and moved by the city of Denton to make room for a city park, now named Quakertown Park. Relocated again, the house is today close to its original site and houses the county's African American Museum chronicling the lives of the county's African American families and the Quakertown experience.

With that history, you would think there would be lingering spirits of those settled and then displaced, but no evidence has surfaced thus far. Still, the house is a place haunted, in a sense, by past history and is certainly worth a visit.

BAYLESS-SELBY HOUSE MUSEUM
317 West Mulberry Street
Denton 76201
(940) 349-2865
www.museumsusa.org/museums/info/1167998

The Bayless-Selby House Museum is also located in Denton's Historical Park, just a short walk from the 1896 Courthouse-on-the-Square. In addition to having this museum and the Quakertown House museum, the park is also home to a welcome center.

Denton's first historic house museum, the Bayless-Selby House dates back to 1884 when Samuel Bayless bought a two-room farmhouse about a mile or so from the county courthouse. Over the years he added on to the farmhouse, transforming it into a two-story Queen Anne–style Victorian structure with a wraparound porch. After Bayless died in 1919, R. L. Selby bought the house, and it stayed in the Selby family until 1970.

Ultimately the city of Denton took it over and finally sold it at auction in 1998 with the stipulation that it must be moved. Mildred Hawk was the successful bidder, and she gave the house to the Denton County Historical Commission so it could become a museum. It opened to the public in 2001. In addition to admiring the architecture, visitors can see the collection of furniture, hand-painted china, and other decorative accessories from the turn of the nineteenth century. Victorian-style gardens, including an antique rose garden, are also on the property.

It would appear that Samuel Bayless moved with the house too, as he is said to show up in and around the house from time to time dressed as the farmer/nurseryman that he was. Perhaps his spirit is restless because he died a violent death. The story is that he got into a heated argument with one of his itinerant workers over payment, and the two moved from exchanging shouted threats to brawling in Bayless's yard. Said to have a quick temper, Bayless entered his house to grab his shotgun. Only after his alarmed wife pointed it out did he realize that his shirt was covered with blood because he had been stabbed during the skirmish. He died before a doctor could be summoned.

THE CAMPUS THEATRE
214 West Hickory Street
Denton 76201
(940) 382-1915
www.campustheatre.com

The Campus Theatre is one of the oldest theaters in North Texas. Built in 1949 in the art deco style, it was a movie theater until 1985. After being closed for ten years, it was refurbished and is now the home of the Denton Community Theater, which features live stage productions. It sits just west of the downtown square and in 2009 was designated a Texas Historic Landmark.

The original general manager of the theater, back in its movie house days, was a man named J. P. Harrison. Community theater volunteers claim he's still around—or at least his spirit is. Mostly they notice sounds like footsteps, but occasionally, they say, the poltergeist plays with the lights. Perceived to be a friendly ghost, he is treated with respect and always referred to as Mr. Harrison. In fact, they hope he makes himself known during rehearsals, as that is likely to ensure a successful performance.

COURTHOUSE-ON-THE-SQUARE
110 West Hickory Street
Denton 76201
(940) 349-2850

Dating back to 1896, the courthouse building is the centerpiece of Denton's downtown square. No longer used as the central place to conduct county business, it now houses the Courthouse-on-the-Square Museum on the first floor. Spirits are more likely to haunt the basement, however, where the public restrooms are, or the second floor, according to anecdotal evidence. Two women on a Ghosts of Denton tour shared a story about the time they beat a hasty retreat, running upstairs from the restrooms because they had a "creepy feeling" that someone was watching them.

Then, of course, there is always the chance that the ghost of John B. Denton, whose grave is on the courthouse lawn, may be wandering about, and locals say the spirits of outlaw Sam Bass and his betrayer Jim Murphy sometimes appear around the square as well.

DOWNTOWN MINI MALL
118 North Locust Street
Denton 76201
(940) 387-0024

Voted Denton's "Best Antique Store" more than once, the Downtown Mini Mall, located on the east side of the square, is fun to wander through even if you are not shopping for antiques or collectibles. Run by a collection of people, more often than not its prices tend toward thrift store rather than high-end antiques figures.

As an added bonus, there's always the chance you might experience a moment with the store's poltergeist, Charlie, who apparently amuses himself by moving things around or maybe looking over a shopper's shoulder.

EMILY FOWLER CENTRAL LIBRARY
502 Oakland Street
Denton 76201
(940) 349-8752
www.cityofdenton.com

Just on the edge of Quakertown Park sits the Emily Fowler Central Library, named for the longtime library director who served from 1943 to 1969. She died in 1971, but some say her spirit still frequents the library. Witnesses claim that she has been known to stack improperly shelved books in the middle of the floor, and a team of paranormal investigators taking readings and recordings for electronic voice phenomena said they heard a faint but definite "shhhhh" when they reviewed the tapes. From the looks and sound of it, she's still on the job.

PATTERSON-APPLETON CENTER FOR THE VISUAL ARTS
400 East Hickory Street
Denton 76201
(940) 382-2787
www.dentonarts.com

Housing the offices of the Greater Denton Arts Council as well as the Center for the Visual Arts, this building on Hickory Street was converted from an old city power plant. It is home to two public art galleries—the Meadows Gallery and the Gough Gallery—and perhaps more than one ghost. Staff members have named one of them Reginald. According to an entry in Shelly Tucker's *Ghosts of Denton* book, a photographer captured Reginald's image one night as she was snapping pictures in the building.

Other reported evidence of ghostly activity are footsteps, murmuring voices in apparent conversation, objects moving, and even full-body apparitions. Tucker does say that since renovations to the building in 2014, "the activity has quieted down quite a bit."

RECYCLED BOOKS
200 North Locust Street
Denton 76201
(940) 566-5688
www.recycledbooks.com

A pastel-painted building northeast from the courthouse square houses one of the largest collections of used books in Texas. Recycled Books has three floors filled with volumes covering a wide variety of genres and topics. It also has CDs and vinyl recordings. Constructed in 1899 with bricks salvaged from Denton's old courthouse, which was condemned after a lightning strike in 1894, the building opened as the Wright Opera House. It was a venue for light opera, melodrama, and vaudeville.

Since 1983, as Recycled Books, the building has been a destination for bibliophiles from all over the state and beyond, including luminaries such as Larry McMurtry, author of *Lonesome Dove* and other best sellers. In 1999 the building was listed on the National Register of Historic Places.

Ghost tour guide Shelly Tucker has collected several stories of spooky encounters from bookstore customers and from residents in the apartments located above the store. They tell of invisible presences that invade personal space or speak, sometimes loudly, throw books off the shelves, or open and close cabinet doors.

DENTON RESTAURANTS

THE ABBEY INN RESTAURANT AND PUB

101 West Hickory Street
Denton 76201
(940) 566-5483
www.theabbeyinndenton.com

Located on Denton's historic courthouse square, The Abbey Inn serves a blend of English favorites, such as bangers and mash or cottage pie, and contemporary American cuisine. Furnished with nineteenth-century church pews and a traditional English bar, the inn features a variety of imported and domestic lagers, ales, and stouts as well as an extensive wine list and an occasional ghost.

One particular ghost is named Seamus, and some patrons have been known to buy a Guinness to put on the table for him. Seamus has a reputation as a bit of a trickster, moving or twirling objects around and causing the bartenders to spill drinks. He may or may not be the source of unexplained footsteps or the shadowy figure some have seen. Then there's the phenomenon of the elevator with doors that open and close and the lift that goes up and down, even though no one is in or near it.

ANDY'S BAR
122 North Locust Street
Denton 76201
(940) 565-5400
www.andys.bar.com

Located in the oldest surviving structure on the square, Andy's Bar advertises that its building has been "a Denton cornerstone since 1876." That's the year it started out as a grocery store owned by B. F. Paschall. Andy's main floor is a full-service bar and grill and a prime music venue. The Basement Bar retains the speakeasy feel left over from its role during Prohibition days. One floor above Andy's is an upscale cocktail lounge called the Paschall Bar—named, of course, for the building's original owner.

The building's ghostly activities reportedly include wailing coming from the walls, smoky odors, doors slamming on their own, and apparitions of a couple of gangsters playing poker or a little girl in a blue dress. Patrons call her Sarah.

HOOLIGANS
104 North Locust Street
Denton 76201
(940) 442-6950
www.hooligansonline.com

A bar and grill featuring a full menu of American fare and a large selection of beers, specialty drinks, and shots, Hooligans is located on Denton's downtown square in a brick-walled 1899 building. Its second floor overlooks the bar, and its patio area offers an impressive view of the historic courthouse. Its twenty flat-screen TVs offer plenty of opportunities for watching sports, and pool and other games are available as well.

As for ghosts, Hooligans has one named Stewart, who is said to whisper only to women—sometimes brushing against or pinching them—and who may be the one whose footsteps sound on the stairs leading to the wraparound second floor. Denton's "Ghost Lady," Shelly Tucker, says people sitting at the bar and looking in the mirror behind it report seeing feet walking on the second-floor walkway behind them. But when they turn around to look, no one is there. Tucker has been told that since she started telling stories about him, Stewart has become even more active.

DENTON ORGANIZED TOURS AND PARANORMAL GROUPS

GHOSTS OF DENTON

Jupiter House Coffee Shop (east side of courthouse square)
106 North Locust Street
Denton 76201
(817) 996-9775
www.ghostsofdenton.com

This haunted history tour of Denton meets on Friday and Saturday nights throughout the year, and tour guide Shelly Tucker is described by *Discover Denton* as one who "leads tour groups around dark Downtown weaving a narrative spell that resurrects the past, uncovers buried secrets, and dusts off forgotten mysteries." A professional storyteller for almost thirty years and a relentless researcher, Tucker is called "The Ghost Lady."

Goatman's Bridge

The Texas state historical marker labels it Old Alton Bridge, but most of the locals call it Goatman's Bridge. It crosses Hickory Creek about 5 miles south of Denton and links two popular hiking and equestrian trails that let you explore the northern tip of Lake Lewisville. Built in 1884, it is described as an iron through-truss bridge, and it takes its official name from the abandoned community of Alton.

Its more common name derives from a story about a man named Oscar Washburn whose spirit, some say, still haunts the site. According to legend, Washburn raised goats on his place just north of the bridge many years ago. He was an African American man with a reputation for being dependable and honest. He prospered and did a modest bit of marketing by putting up a sign on Alton Bridge saying "this way to the Goatman's."

In August 1938, so the story goes, a group of Ku Klux Klansmen objected to the sign and turned to violence. They crossed the bridge with their headlights off, abducted Washburn from his home, and rigged a rope and noose, and hung him off the bridge itself. When they looked down to see if he had died, however, they saw nothing but an empty noose. They returned to his home and burned it to the ground with his family inside. Washburn's body was never found.

In ensuing years, the locals say, it was risky to cross the bridge at night without headlights. You might be met on the other side by the Goatman, or at least see two glowing red eyes if you honked a couple of times. Some visitors daring enough to get out of their cars reported being touched or grabbed or having rocks thrown at them. Abandoned cars in the area and accounts of missing persons added to the lore of paranormal activity.

A concrete-and-steel bridge and a new road replaced the one-lane Alton Bridge in 2001. The old bridge is now closed to vehicle traffic and open only to pedestrian and equestrian traffic on the Elm Fork and Pilot Knoll Hiking and Equestrian Trails, part of the U.S. Corps of Engineers park system. Stories persist, however, of strange noises and mysterious lights in the area.

The bridge was included in the National Register of Historic Places in 1988 and continues to appeal not only to hikers and horseback riders but also to those hoping to encounter a ghost or two. For full disclosure, by the way, there are no records of an Oscar Washburn ever living in Denton County or of a lynching off the Alton Bridge.

If you decide to check it out for yourself, take I-35 East to exit 463 and merge onto the I-35 frontage road. At Lillian Miller Parkway turn right and travel 0.8 mile (at that point, the road becomes FM Road 2181/Teasley Lane); continue 3.2 miles and turn right at Old Alton Road. You will see the bridge on the left.

She continues to add stories to her program and in 2014 published a *Ghosts of Denton* book with the subtitle *The History of the Mysteries in a Small Texas Town*. Her ninety-minute walking tours require advance online registration through the Ghosts of Denton website. Tickets are $15 for adults and $8 for children ages six to eleven; each group is limited to thirty people. Tour groups meet at the Jupiter House at 7:45 p.m., and the tours start promptly at 8:00 p.m. Private tours can be arranged on other nights.

Fort Worth

Fort Worth, affectionately known as "Cowtown" because of its history as the ending point for cattle drives of the Old West, is the fifth-largest city in Texas and the sixteenth-largest in the United States with a population of more than 830,000 people.

It began as a military camp in 1849 and was named after General William Jenkins Worth. The city claims to be the spot in Texas where the West begins, although others claim the same thing. Fort Worth, however, has more proof than most.

Fort Worth grew from a fort into a town and eventually became a thriving city that served as a stop on the Chisholm Trail. It became the center of Texas cattle drives and later served as the hub of the nation's ranching industry.

It was during the height of the cattle drives that an area of town filled with gambling parlors, saloons, and dance halls became known as "Hell's Half Acre." By 1876 the Texas & Pacific Railway connected Fort Worth with the rest of the country, and the city became a premier livestock center.

The Fort Worth Stockyards pays tribute to those days. Once a major center for livestock sales, the Stockyards National Historic District is now a historical tribute to the days of old as well as a major tourist attraction. Art galleries, clothing shops, restaurants, nightclubs, and other commercial businesses can be found in and around the Stockyards.

Don't miss the daily longhorn cattle drive through the Stockyards. You'll also find the Texas Cowboy Hall of Fame here, along with Billy Bob's, the world's largest country-and-western music venue. Downtown is home to a thriving business and entertainment district led by Sundance Square, named for a former visitor by the name of the Sundance Kid.

The Kid and his partner, Butch Cassidy, liked to hang out here. Wyatt Earp and Doc Holliday, who shot it out at the OK Corral, are said to have visited here too. Most of the buildings in Sundance Square date from the turn of the twentieth century. They've been restored to their original architecture and are set amid red-brick streets and verdant courtyards.

As far as ghosts are concerned, Fort Worth is home to a brothel-turned-bed-and-breakfast that is haunted by some of the ladies who once worked there. At another B&B, a ghost likes to climb into bed with women who sleep alone, while a spirit in a downtown hat store likes to move hats around in the business he founded.

It wouldn't be Fort Worth if you didn't have a cowboy ghost or two. So saddle up and head for Cowtown. You probably won't see any cows in this era of the horseless carriage, but you may just encounter a ghost or two.

FORT WORTH ACCOMMODATIONS

MISS MOLLY'S BED AND BREAKFAST HOTEL
109 East Exchange Avenue
Fort Worth 76106
(817) 626-1522
www.missmollyshotel.com

The spirits of ladies of the evening are said to haunt this former bordello. Miss Molly's, located above the Star Cafe in the middle of the Fort Worth Stockyards, was also a boardinghouse but now serves as a bed-and-breakfast.

Witnesses say they have seen apparitions of the former working girls here. They also report unexplained odors, items disappearing and then reappearing, lights switching on and off, toilets flushing for no reason, cold spots, unlocked doors that cannot be opened, and odd sounds.

One housekeeper quit because she kept finding coins in rooms where there had been no guests. Or she would clean a room and return to find coins that she knew had not been there earlier. Geez, how ungrateful! You'd think she would appreciate the extra money.

Miss Molly's, which touts itself as the oldest bed-and-breakfast in Fort Worth, began as a boardinghouse in 1910. Its bordello period occurred in the 1940s, when it operated under the name of Gayatte Hotel.

The seven themed rooms have all been visited by ghosts. Paranormal investigators have visited Miss Molly's too, and copies of their photographs, tape recordings, and written statements of investigators are available for inspection in the common living area.

The rooms are decorated with early twentieth-century antiques. Each room represents a part of the city's past, with cowboy, rodeo, oil industry, and railroad themes. Miss Josie's Room, named after a former madam, is covered in lace. Other rooms are decorated with photos of famous outlaws, old boots, hats, and railroad spikes.

THE STOCKYARDS HOTEL

109 Exchange Avenue
Fort Worth 76106
(800) 423-8471
www.stockyardshotel.com

Cattle barons and their families often stayed at The Stockyards Hotel after it was constructed in 1907. This historic hotel is not far from the haunted Jett Building and Peters Brothers Hats, where you'll find the spirit of the shop's founder.

Colonel Thomas M. Thannisch built The Stockyards Hotel, which, unfortunately, was destroyed by a fire in 1915. A second incarnation was built on the spot and became known as the Chandler Hotel and later the Plaza Hotel.

In 1984 new owners renovated the aging structure and remodeled the interior into the current layout of fifty-two rooms and suites. A second renovation in1996 created a more elegant hotel. The hotel is on the National Register of Historic Places.

The hotel lobby is decorated with western furniture, antiques, and art. Rooms are decorated in four themes described as Victorian, Mountain Man, Cowboy, and Native American. All rooms come with a bath amenities basket and, in the deluxe rooms and suites, an honor snack basket.

Guests have access to workout facilities and a business center.

THE TEXAS WHITE HOUSE

1417 Eighth Avenue
Fort Worth 76104
(817) 923-3597
www.texaswhitehouse.com

All you lonely ladies out there who can't get a man in bed might want to consider a stay at The Texas White House. This white, three-story bed-and-breakfast inn is known for a male ghost who likes to hop into bed with single women. Actually, you don't have to be single; you just have to be alone.

At least two women staying at the inn alone have reported the feeling that someone is in bed with them, according to the website About.com. The ghost is believed to be that of William Newkirk, who purchased the house sometime after 1910. He died in the house in 1957 at the age of ninety-seven.

In one instance, a woman awoke in the middle of the night and had the distinct feeling that someone was lying back to back with her in bed. She lay there for several minutes, too scared to move, until she felt the person get up from the bed. She turned over quickly to see who it was and found no one. Just at that moment, the overhead light came on all by itself.

Another occurrence involved a woman who awoke to the feeling of someone getting into bed with her. Apparently this was not a common event (at least not that she would admit), so she turned immediately to see who it was. No one was there. Just then, her cell phone, which was recharging nearby, beeped for several seconds. The woman said this had never happened before.

This five-room B&B is located near downtown and its museums, entertainment district, historic Stockyards district, and the renowned Bass Performance Hall. The Fort Worth Zoo is also nearby, along with Log Cabin Village and the city's medical district.

Rooms are decorated with antiques and western themes and come with flat-screen HDTVs, premium cable channels, iHome docking stations, free Wi-Fi, hair dryers, irons, and ironing boards. Some rooms come with a CD player, two-person Jacuzzi tub, two-person in-room sauna, balcony porch, living room, and a fireplace.

You won't go hungry at The Texas White House—a gourmet breakfast is served daily. You'll also find early coffee service to your room (upon request), afternoon snacks, and free soft drinks. Spa services are available too. Who knows, maybe the ghost who haunts this place will give you a rubdown.

FORT WORTH ATTRACTIONS
CUTTING EDGE HAUNTED HOUSE
1701 East Lancaster Avenue (intersection of I-30 and U.S. Highway 287)
Fort Worth 76102
(817) 348-8444
www.cuttingedgehauntedhouse.com

Located in a 235,000-square-foot warehouse in downtown Fort Worth, this haunted house claims to be one of the largest ever—a claim backed by the Guinness World Record organization, which declared it to be "The Longest Haunted House in the World" in 2009. It's also been featured on the Travel Channel and was voted by many haunted house rating organizations (including HauntedHouses.com, America Haunts, and Fangoria) for several years as one of the top haunted houses in the country. Built in the 1920s, this warehouse is home each Halloween, and other October nights, to Texas Chainsaw Massacre ghosts, gothic horrors, raging phantoms, and screams that will have you shaking in your cowboy boots.

FORT WORTH ZOO
1989 Colonial Parkway
Fort Worth 76110
(817) 759-7555
www.fortworthzoo.org

The spirit of a former zookeeper crushed and killed by an elephant is said to roam this zoo near the elephant and zebra areas. Another ghost is a woman who appears to be from the late nineteenth century. She is dressed in white, carries a parasol, and walks slowly back and forth near the zoo's cafe.

No one seems to know for sure why the zookeeper hangs around. Perhaps he's still concerned about whether the elephants are being well cared for, or maybe he's plotting his revenge against these weighty pachyderms. Tusk, tusk. Don't be mad. The woman is even more of a mystery. The zoo, the oldest in Texas, opened in 1909, so it's possible she's the ghost of an early visitor.

The Fort Worth Zoo is home to 435 animal species, including 35 that are endangered. This is the only zoo in the nation to house representatives of all four great ape species: gorillas, orangutans, bonobos (pygmy chimps), and chimpanzees. It is also one of five locations in the world to display three of the five rhino species (black, white, and one-horned) in captivity.

The zoo has more than animals. You can also enjoy a carousel, movie, petting zoo, outdoor learning theater, shooting gallery, play area, rock-climbing area, train, and 14,000-square-foot splash park.

THE JETT BUILDING
400 Main Street
Fort Worth 76102
(817) 870-1001

A child who rolls a ball on the second floor and two women who were allegedly murdered here are among the ghosts said to haunt this historic building. Built in 1902, the Jett Building, noted for the Chisholm Trail mural painted on its south side, has been home to several restaurants that failed to make it.

The ghosts here are not known by name, and most of the ghostly activity is what you'd expect. Cold spots, the feeling of being watched or followed, the sound of footsteps, and flickering lights are among them.

The Wlodarskis, in their book *A Texas Guide to Haunted Restaurants, Taverns, and Inns*, report that, in a former restaurant that used to call this building home, lever-operated drink machines would come on by themselves and the "pleading, desperate cries of someone seeking help" could be heard. They also write that a bartender at an earlier former restaurant here once reported seeing the figure of a woman standing in a mirror; a photograph of the building and its boarded-up third-floor windows, when developed, revealed the third-floor windows without boards over them and a human figure standing in a window.

Log Cabin Village
2100 Log Cabin Village Lane
Fort Worth 76109
(817) 926-5881
www.logcabinvillage.org

The scent of lilacs will tell you when you've been joined by a ghost at this living-history museum in Fort Worth. The apparition that haunts the old log cabin on this property is believed to be either the wife of the original owner or a housekeeper who worked for and lived with him.

Lisa Farwell, in her book *Haunted Texas Vacations,* writes that—along with the scent of lilacs—the ghost makes its presence known via a quick drop in temperature and a static charge in the air. Witnesses to this ghost, Farwell writes, describe her as wearing a long black skirt and a high-collared mauve blouse with wide-shouldered leg-of-mutton sleeves.

Log Cabin Village is devoted to preserving Texas history. It includes seven log houses dating to the mid-1800s and an 1870s school. Each is furnished with authentic period artifacts displaying different aspects of pioneer life. Exhibits include a water-powered gristmill, a blacksmith shop, an herb garden, and several log home settings.

Modern-day interpreters dressed in period garb demonstrate nineteenth-century life. Spinners twist wool into thread, a miller grinds shelled corn into meal, and a blacksmith hammers hot metal into various shapes. The village is in a secluded area shrouded by trees and augmented by well-landscaped grounds.

Admire your surroundings and be sure to stop to smell the flowers. Remember, though, it's the smell of lilacs that signals you've been joined by someone from beyond.

PETERS BROTHERS HATS
909 Houston Street
Fort Worth 76102
(817) 335-1715
www.pbhats.com

The spirit of company founder Tom Peters is said to haunt this place. He's not a mean ghost. He enjoys moving hats around the store. Employees and customers alike have gone to fetch a certain hat only to find that it's no longer there. A quick search finds that the hat has been moved, and since no one will fess up to having moved it, the blame naturally falls on Tom.

Tom and his brother, Jim, started the business in 1911. The Greek immigrants saved $600 from shining shoes in Waco and moved to Fort Worth, where they bought a 17-by-10-foot building downtown. They renovated the building and hired four men to shine shoes.

Business grew so much that they expanded the store and hired a total of thirty-six men to shine shoes in two shifts. In addition to the shoe shine business, the Peters Brothers ran a hat "renovation" department, which consisted of cleaning dirty hats. In 1921 Tom moved to Philadelphia to learn to make hats from John B. Stetson, namesake of the famous cowboy hat, and returned to Fort Worth to make hats there.

These popular hats became known as "The Shady Oaks." Today the business is run by grandson Joe Peters, who continues to make "The Shady Oaks" the same way his grandfather did. The store carries a wide variety of hats.

THISTLE HILL HISTORIC HOME
1509 Pennsylvania Avenue
Fort Worth 76104
(817) 336-2344
www.fortworth.com/listings/thistle-hill/5367/

At least two ghosts have been reported at this historic mansion built during the city's cattle baron days. A lady dressed in white has been seen on the grand staircase, and a man with a handlebar mustache and dressed in tennis duds sometimes appears at the top of the stairs. Unexplained music has been heard coming from the home's third-floor ballroom, which has been sealed from visitors, and otherworldly voices have been heard.

The 11,000-square-foot home was built for Electra Waggoner, the daughter of the city's wealthiest cattle baron, A. B. Wharton, who paid $46,000 to have it built. The home is now listed on the National Register of Historic Places and is owned and operated by Historic Fort Worth. The building is open for tours.

Thistle Hill Historic Home includes a two-and-a-half-story main wing with flanking semicircular bays. The home features tall chimneys and a large portico with Tuscan columns. Its red-brick walls are rimmed in cast stone, and the roof consists of beautiful green tile. The interior includes an entry hall with a grand staircase and extensive woodwork.

W. E. Scott Theatre
1300 Gendy Street
Fort Worth 76107
(817) 738-1938

According to the ghosttraveler.com website, a young actor became so distraught one night that he hanged himself from a pipe in the basement of this 500-seat theater. His ghost is now said to spend its time in the basement spooking anyone who comes down there. A wardrobe woman became so frightened by the bizarre laughter coming from the stage one night that she left and never returned.

The W. E. Scott Theatre is designed to serve the city's performing groups. The lobby is decorated with an Italian chandelier 8 feet in diameter and weighing approximately 575 pounds. A mural depicting the history of theater architecture adorns the walls. It includes depictions of ancient Greek and Roman theaters.

So far, there appear to be no reports of the shadowy thespian disturbing performances, but you never know when a ghost will decide to make its presence known.

FORT WORTH RESTAURANTS
Del Frisco's Double Eagle Steak House
812 Main Street
Fort Worth 76102
(817) 877-3999
www.delfriscos.com

The spirit of a man who died from a gunshot wound to the head back in the 1800s is said to haunt the banquet hall and upstairs bar of this Fort Worth restaurant. Del Frisco's is located in the city's downtown area, which used to be known as "Hell's Half Acre" because of its saloons, brothels, and gambling halls. The man whose ghost haunts this place is said to have met his doom in a bathhouse that once stood on this spot.

Del Frisco's is an upscale steak house decorated with rich dark wood, mirrors, soft lighting, and white linen tablecloths. Although reservations are not required, they are recommended. Attire is business casual.

You might want to start with crab cake in Cajun lobster sauce and follow that with a bowl of turtle soup. Then choose from a wide selection of steaks cut from prime, aged, corn-fed beef shipped by truck from the Midwest twice a week.

The Double Eagle Strip, a 26-ounce, bone-in cut, is sure to fill your gullet. If that much meat seems a little over the top, try the 8- or 12-ounce filet mignon.

HUNTER BROTHERS' H3 RANCH
105 East Exchange Avenue
Fort Worth 76164
(817) 624-1246
www.h3ranch.com

The menu for this restaurant next to The Stockyards Hotel is built around grilled meats and homemade sauces. Its hickory wood grill gives meat a special smoked flavor that makes you think you're eating something cooked over a campfire.

The restaurant is named for Robert, David, and William Hunter, who immigrated to the United States from Scotland in the early 1800s. They worked in the cattle business, hunted buffalo, and prospected for gold. You can see photos of them on the walls of this historic restaurant.

H3 Ranch, as it's commonly called, features a variety of steaks, rainbow trout, ribs, chicken, pit-roasted pig, and more.

Ghosts at Spaghetti Warehouse

The Spaghetti Warehouse chain seems to be plagued (or blessed, depending on your attitude) by ghosts. Restaurant locations in Houston and Austin claim to have ghosts hanging around, and the former Fort Worth location on East Exchange Avenue (now home to an energy company) is no exception.

Three ghosts are said to haunt this building in northwest Fort Worth. A small girl has been spotted in the bathroom (the one for women, we hope) turning on water, flushing toilets, and scattering paper towels. Sounds like a job for "Super Nanny"!

Another "woman in white" has been seen on the balcony late at night. No one seems to know her name or why she's there. She doesn't do anything. She's there one minute and gone the next.

In all likelihood the ghost of an old cowboy who used to throw glasses and knock over stools when the building housed the restaurant has had to move on. He'll have to look elsewhere for a barroom brawl these days.

Check out Booger Red's Saloon next door. Named for a champion Texas bronc rider, Booger Red's carries a wide selection of tequilas, beers, and wines.

Start your meal with an order of Nine Miles of Dirt Road, made with layers of seasoned beans, guacamole, sour cream, onion, black olives, and cheddar cheese. It's served with freshly made corn tortilla chips.

H3 Ranch is known for its steaks. The Mexicali steak is a 12-ounce sirloin marinated in H3's wood-roasted salsa and served with two cheese-and-onion enchiladas. Serious steak eaters might want to try the Kansas City strip, a 16-ounce prime beef strip that costs as much as many meals for two.

For dessert, you have your choice of homemade pies, cobblers, and H3's Jack Daniel's ice cream with a brownie and chocolate sauce.

FORT WORTH ORGANIZED TOURS AND PARANORMAL GROUPS

FORT WORTH STOCKYARDS GHOST TOUR

112 West Exchange Avenue
Fort Worth 76164
(817) 616-1011
http://stockyardsghosttour.com

This family-friendly walking tour of the Fort Worth Stockyards is hosted by Cowtown Winery and includes a free beverage that you can enjoy during the tour. A guide takes visitors through the city's historic streets to learn about legendary figures from the city's Wild West days. Butch Cassidy and the Sundance Kid were known to hang out in this area. Wyatt Earp and Doc Holliday, who were part of a legendary gun battle at the OK Corral, in Tombstone, Arizona, are also said to have spent time here. The tour leaves from Cowtown Winery at 112 West Exchange Avenue. The ninety-minute tour costs $20 per adult, $17 for seniors and students, and $10 for children under the age of twelve. Participants are encouraged to bring a camera, because, according to the website, "many people have discovered strange things in the photos they have taken on the tour."

NORTH TEXAS DAY TRIPS AND GETAWAY WEEKENDS

North Texas has something to offer both the day-tripper and the person who wants to get away for a haunted weekend.

The two most haunted cities outside of Dallas and Fort Worth are Arlington and Jefferson. Arlington is smack dab between Dallas and Fort Worth, while Jefferson is a long drive (169 miles) east of Dallas.

First up is **Arlington.** This city of more than 365,000 people is sandwiched between Dallas and Fort Worth, and is home to the Six Flags Over Texas amusement park, Globe Life Park (major league baseball), and the University of Texas at Arlington. The best way to get there from Dallas is to head west on I-30 (also known as Tom Landry Highway); from Fort Worth just head east.

Dungeon of Doom (201 West Main Street, 817-275-4600, www.dungeonofdoomtexas.com), in Arlington, is a permanent fixture in the basement of the Arlington Museum of Art. Proceeds go to support children's art education programs. An ensemble of dedicated actors use headphones to cue one another as they perform "bits" designed to scare the bejeesus out of you. Dungeon of Doom was voted "Best Haunted House" three times by the *Dallas Observer* newspaper and received "5 Bloody Daggers" from the *Fort Worth Star-Telegram.*

River Legacy Parks (701 Northwest Green Oaks Boulevard, 817-459-5473, www.riverlegacy.org), in North Arlington, is said to be the site of quite a bit of ghostly activity. This 1,300-acre park on the Trinity River has 8 miles of paved trails winding through thick forest. Wildlife is abundant in the park; so are ghosts.

One legend has it that a long trail that winds through swamps is haunted by the spirits of Union spies who were hanged from a tree beyond what became known as "Hell's Gate." The spies were led along the trail beneath a canopy of trees through a gate to the hanging tree. Go there today, the legend says, and you'll hear the sobs and prayers of the men who died there.

Then there's the tale of the "screaming bridge." The bridge was the site of a tragic accident involving a head-on collision between a car driven by high school kids celebrating their football team's victory and another car with unknown occupants. Both cars erupted in flames upon collision and plunged over the side of the bridge into the river below.

No one survived.

Legend has it that if you sit on this bridge (the road has been closed to vehicular traffic), you will see the date of the accident and the names of those who died in glowing tombstones that become visible in the water. Once you have the date of the accident, you can return to this bridge on the anniversary. If you do, a heavy fog will rise up from the river, engulfing the bridge and everything on it. You'll gradually begin to see lights shining from either end of the bridge; as the lights grow in intensity, they take on the appearance of headlights headed toward the bridge. The lights remain for a few seconds and then disappear.

The third ghost to haunt this park belongs to a hobo who was spending the night at the park many years ago and was awakened by the sound of screams. He investigated and discovered a parked car and what appeared to be a man and woman fighting inside. As he neared the car, the man hit the woman hard enough to knock her unconscious.

The hobo opened the door and grabbed the man to keep him from hurting the woman even more. They fought until the man pulled out a gun and shot the hobo. The next day, the woman was found wandering the park half naked and delirious, while the hobo was discovered dead on the ground next to where the car had been parked.

To this day, lovers report encounters with the hobo's ghost. They say that if you park there late at night, you'll eventually hear a tapping on your car window, and as you turn toward the sound, you're suddenly face-to-face with the ghost of this long-dead hobo, who is dressed in rags and has a lonely look on his face.

As previously mentioned, Arlington is home to the popular theme park **Six Flags Over Texas** (2201 Road to Six Flags, 817-607-6150, www.sixflags.com/overtexas). The park is set up in six themes reflecting the cultures of the six countries that have flown flags over Texas throughout its history.

In the Texas section next to the park entrance to the Texas Giant (a wooden roller coaster), a candy store painted in yellow is home to the ghost of an eight-year-old girl. "Annie" is believed to have drowned in a nearby creek in the early 1900s. She haunts this building, which is believed to be the oldest in the park, and the nearby railroad tracks.

She has been spotted on the tracks or in the house opening and closing curtains and turning lights on and off. Security guards say Annie gives them trouble at night when they go to lock the door to the candy store's upstairs section. Annie fiddles with the lock while they try to secure it, making the job much more difficult than normal.

Arlington also is home to **Globe Life Park** (1000 Ballpark Way, 817-273-5100). Home to the Texas Rangers baseball team, this 49,000-seat stadium is considered one of the best baseball parks in the country. The team plays from April to September.

Need a place to stay? Try the **Hilton Arlington** (2401 East Lamar Boulevard, 817-640-3322), or the **Howard Johnson Express Inn** (2001 East Copeland Road, 817-461-1122). You'll find plenty of restaurants in the Six Flags/Globe Life Park area. Two you might want to try are **The Cacharel** (2221 East Lamar Boulevard, 9th floor, 817-640-9981, http://cacharel .net), for fine dining, and **Mariana's Mexican Cuisine** (2614 Majesty Drive, 817-640-5118, www.laharanch.com).

Jefferson is a two-and-a-half-hour drive from Dallas and 20 miles from the Louisiana state line. This part of the state doesn't resemble what most people think of when they think of Texas.

This town of around 2,000 people is not a city steeped in memories of cowboys and ranchers. Instead, it's a town that owes its existence to lumberjacks, riverboat captains, and dock workers. The area in and around Jefferson is characterized by swamps, bayous, and alligators. It became part of the U.S. territories after the 1803 Louisiana Purchase.

Jefferson may have more ghosts than it does people.

One of the best known haunted places is the **Jefferson Hotel** (124 West Austin Street, 903-665-2631, http://historic jeffersonhotel.com). This twenty-five-room hotel is decorated in Victorian furniture, and town residents enjoy sharing the ghost stories related to it.

Those who have worked or stayed at the Jefferson Hotel say it's common to hear whispers, knocking on walls, and orchestra music coming from a closed dining hall. They also report the smell of cigar smoke, faucets coming on by themselves, and doors that pull back when someone tries to pull them shut.

Hear that clickety-clack sound of shoes against hardwood floors? It's coming from the hall. The problem is, the halls are carpeted. Hear the children laughing and playing in the middle of the night? Hear the child calling for its mother, a baby crying? There aren't any kids staying at the hotel! Feel someone's eyes on you? Get used to it. The ghosts are always watching.

See that thick, white cloud? See the thin blonde with long tresses in the middle of it? She's a ghost. An elderly man once spotted the woman floating down the stairs to the lobby one early morning, disappearing before she reached the bottom step.

A former desk clerk who was ending his shift one night once reported that the doors to the second floor began opening and slamming shut all at once. He also heard the sound of footsteps and someone dragging furniture across the floor. This might have been explained as some sort of prank played by a hotel guest except for one thing: The desk clerk was alone in the building. Or was he?

Guests have reported being awakened at night by the frosty touch of a petite woman, bathroom spigots turning on in the middle of the night, the sound of scraping and banging, and the echoes of someone crying.

The Excelsior House (211 West Austin Street, 903-665-2513, www.theexcelsiorhouse.com) is located across the street from the Jefferson Hotel. It, too, is haunted. This historic hotel was built in the 1850s from brick and timber and lacy ironwork. It's furnished with rosewood, cherry, and mahogany pieces. Ulysses S. Grant, Oscar Wilde, Rutherford B. Hayes, and Lady Bird Johnson have reportedly stayed at the hotel.

So, apparently, have several others, whose restless spirits still roam the two-story hotel. One of these ghosts is said to be the spirit of a headless man (or is it a headless spirit?) who inhabits the second floor, scaring the heck out of anyone who happens upon him. Another ghost is a woman in black who has been spotted with a baby—a ghost baby!

Rumor has it that filmmaker Stephen Spielberg, who was in the area making the movie *Sugarland Express*, once stayed at the hotel and became so frightened by the ghosts that he checked out.

Morgan Cattle Restaurant (121 West Austin Street, 903-601-5061) is said to be haunted by a host of ghosts. One is believed to be the spirit of an African American man hanged for a crime he did not commit. Another ghost or ghosts may belong to the prostitutes who once used the second floor of this building to ply their trade.

Employees report hearing their names being whispered, of bumping into an invisible presence, and losing things only to find them later in unusual places.

Another haunted restaurant is **Lamache's Italian Restaurant** (124 West Austin Street, 903-665-6177). The restaurant is adjacent to the Jefferson Hotel and connected by double doors. Employees have reported hearing the sound of Big Band music coming from the restaurant. They've also heard knocking on the connecting doors. They say candles flicker, the electrical system malfunctions regularly, and the sound of wine glasses clinking together is common.

Jefferson is also home to **Terror on the Bayou** (1602 Highway 49 East, 903-665-6464, www.terroronthebayou.com)—three frightening attractions all at one site. The Creepy Screamin' Maze, the Runaway Fright Train, and the Haunted Forest Walk will scare the daylights out of you, in a fun way of course.

The Creepy Screamin' Maze is a post-apocalyptic wasteland set in a corn maze. Not only do you have to find your way out, but you also have to avoid horrific-looking "survivors" (live actors) who add to the horror. The Runaway Fright Train is a haunted house on wheels that travels 5 miles along the tracks of the Jefferson & Cypress Bayou Railway. The Haunted Forest Walk is a trek through a cypress bayou, complete with a 100-foot Tunnel of Doom. Terror on the Bayou runs during the last three weeks of October every year; check the website for schedules, fees, directions, and the scare-factor rating of each attraction.

WEST TEXAS

Abilene

The Abilene Convention and Visitors Bureau folks like to say that in this west-central Texas city, "the frontier spirit lives on." It is "a place where western heritage is both a birthright and a pastime." Located about 150 miles southwest of Fort Worth, it is the twenty-seventh most populous city in the state and the hub of a nineteen-county area commonly known as "The Big Country."

Its beginnings are tied to cattle and cattlemen, some of whom established the town as a stock shipping point on the Texas & Pacific Railway in 1881. It is named after Abilene, Kansas, where cattle drives on the Chisholm Trail ended. The Frontier Texas! multimedia museum highlights the area's heritage from 1780 to 1880.

Between 1891 and 1923 three universities were established here: Hardin-Simmons University, Abilene Christian University, and McMurry University. In addition, Abilene now has branches of Cisco Junior College, Texas State Technical College, and Texas Tech University.

Among the three lakes in the city, at least one, Fort Phantom Lake, is said to be haunted. An ambitious revitalization of the downtown area in the 1980s included restorations of some of the city's historic buildings and possibly stirred up some ghosts as well. Mysterious lights and intriguing apparitions are all part of the lure and lore of Abilene.

ABILENE ACCOMMODATIONS

COURTYARD ABILENE NORTHEAST AND TOWNEPLACE SUITES

2141 Scottish Road
Abilene 79601
(325) 673-0400
www.marriott.com

Two Marriott properties in Abilene share the same address and some of the same amenities with the idea of attracting both business travelers and tourists. The seventy-six-room Courtyard Abilene Northeast features on-site dining at The Bistro and offers free Wi-Fi and parking. The fitness center, heated outdoor pool, and meeting space are shared with the seventy-six-unit TownePlace Suites, designed for longer stays. There guests can enjoy a complimentary hot breakfast buffet and spread out in studio suites with fully equipped kitchens and separate living/working and sleeping areas. The hotels are convenient to Abilene Christian University and downtown attractions.

HAMPTON INN AND SUITES

3526 West Lake Road
Abilene 79601
(325) 673-4400
www.hamptoninn3.hilton.com

One of the hotels on I-20 located closest to Fort Phantom Hill, the Hampton Inn and Suites is convenient to other area attractions also. It has an outdoor pool, a fitness facility, a hot/cold breakfast buffet, a business center, and free parking and Wi-Fi. Its lobby features western art and a fireplace, and amenities in each room or suite include a minifridge, microwave, and premium cable television.

SAYLES LANDMARK
642 Sayles Boulevard
Abilene 79605
(325) 670-9402
www.sayleslandmark.com

The historic Sayles Landmark was built in 1889 and is one of the oldest houses in Abilene. Listed on the National Register of Historic Places, it is now a six-room upscale bed-and-breakfast close to the city center.

The Queen Anne Victorian structure was the original family home of Judge Henry Sayles. Its architectural history is complemented by modern accommodations providing comfort and privacy for guests. Breakfast is served in the century-old carriage house, and there are a number of public spaces to visit and explore. You'd think there might be ghosts as well, but nary a one has been reported so far.

SUPER 8 ABILENE SOUTH
4397 Sayles Boulevard
Abilene 79605
(325) 701-4779
www.super8.com

This budget hotel off U.S. Highway 84 is 4 miles from downtown Abilene and 10 miles from Buffalo Gap Historic Village. It is pet friendly and offers a continental breakfast, an outdoor swimming pool, and free parking and Wi-Fi.

TRAVEL INN
2202 West Overland Trail
Abilene 79603
(325) 677-2463

Reviewers give this budget inn a spooky rating for more than just ghostly reasons, but stay if you dare. It is said to be haunted, although no one seems to know why. Reports are that lights go on and off late at night, strange noises are heard, and objects get moved around. An apparition of a man in a green coat wanders the hallways and moves around the office in the early hours of the morning.

Less eerie are the expected amenities: outdoor pool, gym, restaurant, business center, and free Wi-Fi and parking. Located near Hardin Simmons University, the Travel Inn is less than 4 miles from downtown. Pets are allowed.

WHITTEN INN UNIVERSITY
1625 Texas Highway 351
Abilene 79601
(325) 673-5271
www.whitteninn.com/locations/whitten-inn-university

This no-frills motel-style lodging offers free breakfast, Wi-Fi, and parking. As its name suggests, it is very close to Abilene Christian University and Hardin Simmons University and a little less than 3 miles from the city center and Frontier Texas!

Like the Travel Inn described above, it is said to be home to strange sights and even smells. Bathroom lights go on and off by themselves, objects disappear and then reappear under the bed, and sudden malodorous smells occur early in the morning. Some witnesses have reported seeing an apparition of a red-bearded man in green clothing in the office. Could it be the same green-coated man who wanders the hallways at the Travel Inn?

ABILENE ATTRACTIONS
FORT PHANTOM HILL
10818 FM 600
Abilene 79601
(325) 677-1309
www.fortphantom.org

All that remains of Fort Phantom Hill today are three stone buildings and dozens of stone chimneys. And possibly a ghost or two.

One of a second line of forts laid out in the 1850s to protect westward-moving pioneers settling in Texas or continuing on to the goldfields in California, its remains are part of the Texas Forts Trail, a 650-mile highway tour of historic Texas forts in the west-central part of the state. It was originally known as the Post on the Clear Fork of the Brazos and was occupied by the U.S. Army from 1851 until 1854.

After the fort was abandoned, fires destroyed the post's log and adobe structures, and only the tall stone chimneys were left standing. Three of the original stone buildings—a powder magazine, a guardhouse, and a commissary/warehouse—survived as well.

As you might guess, the fort's name change resulted from eerie circumstances very early on. One is an apparent topographical phenomenon. The hill on which the fort was built rises sharply from the plains then seems to level out as it is approached, vanishing like a phantom. A more ghostly version of the story says a nervous sentry shot at an apparition he thought was the spirit of an American Indian, possibly a Comanche, and reported seeing a phantom on the hill. Other stories derive from speculation that other restless Native American ghosts from frontier times continue to stalk their former hunting grounds during the night. Still another legend says that an innocent man wrongly hanged near the fort haunts the place, and that his accusers all died in mysterious ways.

Described on its website as "one of the most pristine historic sites in Texas," Fort Phantom Hill is open to visitors daily dawn until dusk. Access is free, and informational brochures enable visitors to explore the site on self-guided tours. Ample parking and public restrooms are available.

FRONTIER TEXAS!
625 North First Street
Abilene 79601
(325) 437-2800
www.frontiertexas.com

It is through technology that the Frontier Texas! history museum brings the dead to life, in the form of holograms in its exhibits. Called "spirit guides," these life-size holographic figures—eight of them—represent real people from different segments of the frontier population returning to tell their stories. Visitors may get some sense of a wolf attack, a buffalo stampede, and a deadly card game shootout, among other experiences at the museum. They meet, at least figuratively, buffalo hunters, Comanche warriors and captives, explorers, and pioneers. In addition to providing audiovisual and interactive experiences for visitors, Frontier Texas! serves as the visitor center for the city of Abilene and the Texas Forts Trail region. A general store is also on-site, featuring Texas-themed gifts.

GRACE MUSEUM
102 Cypress Street
Abilene 79601
(325) 673-4587
www.thegracemuseum.org

Built originally as the Hotel Grace in 1909 and later existing as the Drake Hotel, the repurposed Grace Museum now houses five art galleries featuring rotating art exhibitions and artwork from its permanent collection, plus a history gallery with artifacts that tell the story of the evolving cultural and social history of the area in the late nineteenth and twentieth centuries. It also has an art library, an education center, and an interactive gallery for children and families.

The four-story building sat vacant for almost fifteen years before preservation groups rallied to save it from demolition and convert it from a hotel into a museum. It and the Paramount Theater became the centerpieces for the downtown revitalization of Abilene in the mid-1980s. Prior to its restoration the Grace building had fallen into disrepair and was inhabited by rats, cats, and homeless vagrants. Some say that ghosts are there too—spirits from the past that never left. They offer as evidence the sounds of footsteps and other noises, heard mostly at night, and the sight of doorknobs that turn by themselves. The reported paranormal activity seems to be concentrated on the third and fourth floors or in the ballroom and the basement. The Southwest Ghost Hunters Association has explained away most of the phenomena but did locate some electromagnetic fields in those areas.

HILL HOUSE IN BUFFALO GAP HISTORIC VILLAGE
133 William Street
Buffalo Gap 79508
(325) 572-3365
www.buffalogap.com

Hill House is one of the twenty-plus buildings gathered at Buffalo Gap Historic Village, 6 miles south of Abilene. Originally located in Abilene in the late 1880s, the house was home to

Abilene's first marshal, Tom Hill, and his family. Some say Tom's spirit moved with the house to Buffalo Gap, and they're even more convinced that his daughter Belle is still around. The rumor is that she doesn't like men.

After the house was moved to Buffalo Gap in 1964 and opened to the public, visitors and workers began to describe strange goings-on. One man visiting the house said he saw, out of the corner of his eye, just the half figure of a woman. Maintenance workers tell of a gun cabinet slamming shut, and one supervisor got goosebumps because of buttons. He had picked up a white mother-of-pearl button off the floor one day and put it in his pocket. He forgot about it and took it home. The next morning he found it under his pillow. Another time he set his drill down and walked away to make other repairs. When he came back, a vintage pewter button was sitting on the drill.

Members of the West Texas Paranormal Society were invited to lead a night ghost hunt in the village. The strongest signal they picked up, they said, was in Hill House from an old woman who did not care for men.

As for Tom, he's more likely to make himself known by creating cold spots, touching a visitor's hair, or even speaking. No one is sure about who might be leaving the buttons, although Belle is suspected, but several visitors have claimed to find an antique button in a pocket when they got home.

Lake Fort Phantom Hill

FM 600–Westlake Road
Abilene 79601
(325) 676-6218 (City of Abilene)
tpwd.texas.gov/fishboat/fish/recreational/lakes/fort_phantom/

North of downtown Abilene on Elm Creek in Jones County is Lake Fort Phantom Hill, 2 miles south of the fort for which it is named.

A man-made lake, it didn't come along until 1938, but it has its phantoms too. Anglers are more likely to come hoping to catch blue catfish, hybrid striped bass, largemouth bass, or white crappie rather than to encounter ghostly spirits. Nevertheless, legends abound and keep the curious intrigued.

The most prevalent stories center on the "lady of the lake," although not everyone agrees on who she might be. Some say that a pioneer couple built a small cabin in what was then Comanche country (the Comancheria). The husband and wife agreed on a secret password, and neither was to admit anyone who did not offer the code word at the door. In fact, the one inside the cabin was to shoot anyone or anything that tried to enter. One day the husband went out hunting and got ambushed and wounded by Comanche warriors. He managed to escape and get back to the cabin, where he began clawing at the door. Either because of his wounds or his state of mind, he neglected to utter the password. His wife shot and killed him while he was still on the stoop. In her remorse she became cursed to wander the area for eternity and was showing up even before the lake existed.

Two other legends date back to the 1940s and mention the lake specifically. In one tale a young couple was to meet at the church to exchange wedding vows. The groom did not arrive. The next morning authorities found his body in a boat floating in the middle of the lake. He was dressed in his best suit and showed an expression of severe pain on his face. His murderer was never found, and some say the spirit of his fiancée continues to search for the killer.

In yet another story a woman is the victim of murder. Some say her name was Mona Bell. She and her lover, a young soldier returning from war, agreed to meet at the lake, where he would signal her by flashing his headlights three times. When she arrived, she ran to meet her beloved only to encounter an enraged man who had been told, jokingly, by a friend that the friend had been keeping company with Mona while the soldier was away. The angry young lover didn't get the joke and put his hands around the woman's neck to throttle her and throw her in the lake. Some reports say she was not dead when she hit the water, but screamed and made gurgling sounds as she drowned. In this version it is the murdered woman who wanders the lake.

Others connect her to the La Llorona story of a woman searching for her drowned children who died by her own hand.

Whatever the backstory, the phantom woman is sometimes said to be dressed in a long, light-colored dress or gown or robe as she wanders aimlessly. Or she's said to be only a vague apparition floating over the lake, sometimes carrying a lantern and surrounded by a bluish glow. She may make herself known by causing your headlights to flicker when you drive by the lake, or she may surround your car with a dense fog.

Some say she has also been seen at the nearby Fort Phantom Hill Cemetery. Other paranormal activities around the lake are sounds of screams, moaning, gunshots, and rapping against vehicle windows. There's also the smell of decaying fish or perfume and roses.

Visitors who might want to stay overnight to look for ghosts should know that in addition to day-use areas and boat ramps around the lake, there are spaces for primitive camping at two city parks: Seabee and Johnson Park. No fees are required.

ABILENE RESTAURANTS
ABUELO'S
4782 South 14th Street
Abilene 79605
www.abuelos.com

Tex-Mex, steaks, and barbecue are three staples in a Texan's diet, and Abuelo's serves up plenty of the first on the list. Part of a Texas-based chain serving Mexican food and margaritas in a hacienda-style setting, the restaurant in Abilene gets high marks for its food and service. Efficient but not "fast food" focused, Abuelo's boasts made-from-scratch dishes including salsas, sauces, sides, and hand-rolled enchiladas.

BEEHIVE RESTAURANT & SALOON
442 Cedar Street
Abilene 79601
(325) 675-0600
www.beehivesaloon.com

Earning a "best country steakhouse in the state" designation from *Texas Monthly* magazine, the Beehive is a destination for anyone hankering for aged Angus beef steaks. Seafood and chicken entrees are also on the menu at this upscale eatery with an Old West flair. Carnivores can choose from 10- to 14-ounce filet mignons, rib eyes, or New York strips, and seafood selections range from shrimp and smoked salmon to red snapper, tilapia, and orange roughy. Reviewers praise not only the food but also the service.

BELLE'S CHICKEN DINNER HOUSE
2002 North Clack Street
Abilene 79603
(325) 677-7100

If you are looking for a Southern-inspired, family-style, home-cooked meal amid West Texas ambience, Belle's Chicken Dinner House is the place to go. As you would expect, there is an array of chicken dishes as well as chicken-fried steak, fried catfish, rib eye, and home-style sides like mashed potatoes and gravy. Diners rave about the homemade yeast rolls served with honey and butter, and often save room for desserts such as homemade pies or warm banana pudding with meringue.

JOE ALLEN'S PIT BBQ
301 South 11th Street
Abilene 79602
(325) 672-6082

Although moved from its original location, this laid-back restaurant is an Abilene icon. It has earned a "best steak and barbecue" Readers' Choice Award among the locals. Familiar barbecue plates and classic sides are on the menu, as are steaks and seafood. Mesquite-smoked briskets are cooked for eighteen hours or more until they are fork tender. Joe Allen's also caters.

PERINI RANCH STEAKHOUSE
3002 FM 89
Buffalo Gap 79508
(325) 572-3339
www.store.periniranch.com

It's worth the drive to have lunch or dinner at this acclaimed eatery just south of Abilene. It is best known for its mesquite-grilled beef cuts and Southern comfort food served in a converted hay barn. Other menu offerings range from quail legs and jalapeño bites as appetizers to shrimp, catfish, or chicken entrees to bread pudding, strawberry shortcake, or jalapeño cheesecake for dessert. The restaurant has earned accolades from *Texas Monthly* magazine and NBC's *Today* show and has catered a Congressional picnic at the White House. Reservations are recommended.

224

The Anson Lights

About 20 miles north of Abilene is the small town of Anson. Ghost hunters drive there hoping to see the Anson Lights. As is the case with most ghost legends, this one has a story.

A woman living back in the 1800s had a child—or children—who failed to return home one evening, and she continues to look for them. One tale says there were three sons sent to chop wood and told to flash their lantern three times if they encountered any trouble. They did. But by the time the mother reached them, they had been killed. Other stories move the time frame up to the Depression era and say that only one boy or maybe a girl got lost in a snowstorm. In any case the mother, carrying a lantern, went looking for the lost offspring, and now her ghost continues the search, especially if drivers flash their car lights three times.

For those seeking to see the Anson Lights, the directions are specific: From Anson, take U.S. Highway 180 east to Mount Hope Cemetery. Turn right at the county road by the cemetery and drive about a mile until you reach a crossroad. At the crossroad turn your car back toward the cemetery and flash your headlights three times. That action is believed to bring the spirit of the mother still carrying her lantern in search of her child/children, and the Anson Lights then appear.

Actually, only a single white light begins to travel slowly down the road toward you, observers say, sometimes swaying, dancing, or changing size or color. Some locals

(*continued*)

claim that the light appears only on warm, clear nights, calling into question the stories about the blizzard.

Skeptics, including a professor and his students from an Abilene Christian University experimental psychology class in 2011, have debunked the ghost theory and tried to prove the lights are nothing more than car headlights from southbound traffic on nearby U.S. Highway 277. Earlier the Southwest Ghost Hunters Association had arrived at the same theory. But the true believers are having none of it, so you'll just have to go see for yourself and reach your own conclusions.

ABILENE ORGANIZED TOURS AND PARANORMAL GROUPS

BUFFALO GAP HISTORIC VILLAGE ANNUAL GHOST TOURS
133 William Street
Buffalo Gap 79508
(325) 572-3365
www.buffalogap.com

Every year in October this historic frontier-town complex of buildings from the 1880s to 1920s is the site of ghost tours. Every ten minutes a tour leaves from the reportedly haunted Hill House and stops in several of the other village buildings where members of the Mesquite Storytellers spin a few yarns. Visitors are lured in with questions such as: Will the jail cell lock behind you in the old Taylor County Courthouse? Does Belle still haunt the village?

HAUNTED ABILENE TOUR
1726 Swenson Street
Abilene 79603
(325) 676-3775
www.hauntedabilene.com

The weekend before Halloween each year, the Abilene Preservation League sponsors two nights of family-friendly fun at the Swenson House. The historic mansion is decorated as the headquarters of the Creepy Clown Circus, and a trolley ghost tour leaves from there throughout the evening, cruising the streets of Abilene with the conductor and actors telling tales of history and spirits. Proceeds go to support historic preservation and conservation in Abilene.

El Paso

The folks at the tourism bureau in El Paso tout this city of 700,000 as a "two-nation, three-state" destination where visitors can "see Texas and taste Mexico." Located in a pass between the Franklin Mountains, El Paso is at the western tip of Texas where Texas, New Mexico, and Mexico meet.

The city is just across the border from the Mexican city of Juarez and its 1.5 million residents, while New Mexico is a short drive from anywhere in the city. El Paso is the largest international metroplex in the world, a place where three cultures blend together.

Spanish conquistadores first discovered this area in 1598. The mountains, which cut through the middle of the city, offer an attractive vista. The Wyler Aerial Tramway to Ranger Peak is a great way to get a bird's-eye view of the area. It takes riders on a ride 946 feet up the mountain. At the top you can see 7,000 square miles.

The sun shines in El Paso for an average of 305 days a year. You won't see many ghosts when the sun is out, but come nightfall things start to change. It gets a whole lot cooler, for one thing, because the desert-like terrain doesn't hold in the heat the way it does in other types of climates.

El Paso has a couple of historic cemeteries that are haunted, as well as an art museum. You might encounter the phantom of a monk and his donkey as you're driving through the mountains. Enjoy dinner at a restaurant that overlooks the Rio Grande, where you could hear the wails of a woman's ghost searching for her dead children.

EL PASO ACCOMMODATIONS
CAMINO REAL EL PASO
101 South El Paso Street
El Paso 79901
(915) 534-3000
www.caminoreal.com/elpaso

This high-rise hotel in downtown El Paso is a few blocks from the haunted El Paso Museum of Art and just a few more blocks from the border. There's something about staying in a hotel built in the early 1900s (or earlier) that makes ghost hunting all the more fun.

Built in 1912, the Camino Real is both elegant and warm. Its sandy-colored exterior fits right in with El Paso's arid terrain. Listed on the National Register of Historic Places, it offers 359 rooms and suites and claims to have the most photographed grand staircase in the Southwest.

The lobby and ballrooms are decorated with crystal chandeliers, and the hotel is accented with marble that was cut and polished by skilled Italian craftsmen almost a century ago. The hotel offers two restaurants: Azulejos (regional Mexican food) and Dome Restaurant (fine dining).

Hotel amenities include the Dome Bar fitted with an original Tiffany glass dome, a swimming pool and fitness center, a gift shop, free transportation, and a business center. Room amenities include cable TV, air-conditioning, a free daily newspaper, iron, in-room complimentary Wi-Fi, and a coffee/tea maker.

CHASE SUITE HOTEL
6791 Montana Avenue
El Paso 79925
(915) 772-8000
www.chasehotelelpaso.com

You'll find one- and two-bedroom suites at this economically priced hotel. It's located in the northeast part of town not far from the airport, Fort Bliss, and the Loretto Academy's ghostly nun. Each of its 200 suites comes with fully equipped kitchens, a living room area, cable TV with premium channels, nice bathrooms, and high-speed Internet access.

Each morning, Chase Suites provides guests with a continental breakfast buffet, and Monday through Thursday you can enjoy the "evening social hour" with drinks and hors d'oeuvres. Hotel amenities include free parking, two swimming pools, a whirlpool spa, and free shuttle service. Room amenities include coffeemakers, high-speed Internet access, LCD TVs, hair dryers, microwave ovens, refrigerators, and AM/FM clock radios. A limited number of rooms with fireplaces are available.

HOLIDAY INN EXPRESS—CENTRAL
409 East Missouri Avenue
El Paso 79901
(915) 544-3333
www.ihg.com

This red-and-yellow high-rise remodeled in 2005 has a modern look to it while paying homage to the region's Mexican culture and its vivid colors. The Holiday Inn is a moderately priced hotel in downtown El Paso, which brings you close to the border and the haunted Plaza Theatre.

The Hatchet Lady

Unrequited love is a common theme in ghost stories. Many jilted lovers are said to haunt the place where they received the unfortunate news that their beloved had decided not to marry them after all.

Women seem to suffer most from these events, especially those who are left at the altar on their wedding days. But one woman in West Texas took the news very hard long before the wedding day came around.

It supposedly occurred in Buie Park near a small town called Stamford in West Texas. A woman whose name has not been recorded by history went to the park with her fiancé to relax and discuss their impending nuptials.

The young woman, glowing with love for her fiancé and romantic thoughts of their wedding day, was devastated when her fiancé informed her that he had decided not to marry her after all. Devastated, the woman flew into a rage and in a moment of passion killed her lover with a hatchet.

The legend doesn't explain where the hatchet came from. Had the groom brought it along to chop wood for a fire, or did the bride simply have a fondness for sharp objects? No one knows, but the hatchet turned out to be an effective and convenient way for the bride to express her displeasure.

Not only did the disappointed bride bury a hatchet in her lover's head, but she also probably kept the ring. After all, how could the groom return it once he'd been killed?

You might expect the groom to haunt this park. Not so.

The park is haunted instead by the bride, whose unbridled hatred for her former lover—and love in general—is

(continued)

manifested whenever a young couple goes to this abandoned park to be alone.

Couples seeking some privacy in this empty place find their passion rudely interrupted by a hatchet-wielding woman intent on ruining their amorous adventures. Needless to say, she is successful, for who among us can concentrate on love while a ghost with an affinity for hatchets is standing outside our car window?

Its 110 rooms come with cable TV, clock radios, hair dryers, irons and ironing boards, dataports, free high-speed Internet access, coffeemakers, and in-room safes. Like many hotels in El Paso, the view from most windows is tremendous, with the Franklin Mountains, Juarez, and El Paso spread out before you.

Hotel amenities include a free breakfast, restaurant, lounge, fitness center, guest laundry, heated pool, and business center.

La Quinta Inn
7620 North Mesa Street
El Paso 79912
(915) 585-2999
www.lq.com

This hundred-room hotel offers a great view of the Franklin Mountains. It's also conveniently located near the Woodrow Bean Transmountain Drive and its spectral monk and donkey.

Located north of downtown, this La Quinta is 8 miles from the airport, which by highway should take no more than fifteen minutes. Hotel amenities include free breakfast, parking, and local calls; a swimming pool; and wheelchair-accessible rooms.

Rooms come with coffeemakers, dataports, hair dryers, irons and ironing boards, voice mail, in-room movies, and high-speed Internet access.

SUNSET HEIGHTS BED & BREAKFAST INN
717 West Yandell Street
El Paso 79902
(915) 544-1743

Those who enjoy bed-and-breakfast inns and want to be near the downtown area and its haunted destinations will want to give Sunset Heights Bed & Breakfast Inn a try. It's just a mile from downtown. This three-story Victorian home built in 1905 is encircled by a wrought-iron fence that gives it a stately appearance.

Public rooms are on the first floor. Three guest rooms, each with a private bath, occupy the second floor. The third floor can be reserved for conferences. Breakfast is worth the stay alone. The proprietors serve five to eight tasty courses each morning. Outside, enjoy the swimming pool, Jacuzzi, and fireplace.

The Sunset Heights B&B is within walking distance of downtown El Paso and the University of Texas. Walk through the Sunset Heights neighborhood and enjoy the collection of Victorian homes, many of which have been refurbished to their original luster.

EL PASO ATTRACTIONS
CONCORDIA CEMETERY
3700 West Yandell Street
El Paso 79901
(915) 842-8200
www.concordiacemetery.org

It's been said that at night you can hear the sounds of children laughing and playing in this cemetery. Scores of children died and were buried here in the 1800s as the result of a smallpox epidemic. Listen closely and you might also hear the sound of U.S. Cavalry soldiers galloping toward you. Sometimes you can hear them talking.

The cemetery, founded around 1840, began as a ranch settled by pioneers Hugh Stephenson and his wife, Juana Maria Ascarate. The Concordia Heritage Association maintains the site, which is home to the graves of Chinese immigrants who came to America to build the railroads. Buffalo soldiers, the nickname originally given by Native Americans to African American soldiers who fought with U.S. Army cavalry regiments, also are buried here.

The cemetery is open to the public, and signs have been posted to help visitors find the graves of important historical figures.

EL PASO MUSEUM OF ART
1 Arts Festival Plaza
El Paso 79901
(915) 532-1707
www.elpasoartmuseum.org

An old woman has been spotted several times looking out at passersby from an upper-level window in the El Paso Museum of Art. Lights sometimes flicker for no apparent reason, and doors open and close by themselves. Moans have also been heard coming from the basement.

The El Paso Museum of Art is located near the boundary of Texas, Mexico, and New Mexico. The museum is home to a permanent collection of more than 5,000 works of art, including the Samuel H. Kress Collection of European art from the thirteenth through eighteenth centuries, American art from the nineteenth and twentieth centuries, and Mexican colonial art and *retablos* (frames enclosing painted panels) from the eighteenth and nineteenth centuries. The museum also displays temporary exhibits and sponsors films, lectures, concerts, and other educational programs.

EVERGREEN CEMETERY
4301 Alameda Street
El Paso 79905
(915) 532-5511

This forty-seven-acre cemetery dates back to 1894. Drive by the cemetery in the early morning hours and you'll eventually see a boy standing on the sidewalk out in front looking for a ride. By the time you stop—assuming you have the courage—the boy has disappeared.

Take a hike to the back of the cemetery near the railroad tracks and you might encounter the mysterious mist that sometimes rises up from the unknown. According to the website www.unexplainable.net, you'll also be hit by a strong odor that is neither pleasant nor unpleasant, and has yet to be aptly described by anyone.

FORT BLISS
Pershing and Pleasanton Streets
Fort Bliss 79916
(915) 568-2121
www.bliss.army.mil

This U.S. Army base in northeast El Paso is one of the country's largest. It's home to the annual Amigo Air Show (held each September), fairs, four museums, and one of the biggest PXs in the Southwest.

The Fort Bliss Museum and Study Center chronicles the post's history from its early days as a regiment of mounted infantry to its present expansiveness. The museum houses the Air Defense Artillery Gallery, devoted to the introduction of the airplane as an offensive weapon in World War I.

The Old Fort Bliss Museum re-creates the fort as it appeared from 1854 to 1868. Exhibits allow visitors a look into the olden days via period-room exhibits and outdoor displays. The U.S. Army Museum of the Noncommissioned Officer features the story of the changing role of the noncommissioned officer from 1775 to the present. Equipment and uniforms used by sergeants and other NCOs are on display. Admission to both museums is free.

JUAREZ, MEXICO

One of the main reasons people enjoy visiting El Paso is its proximity to Mexico and the city of Juarez just across the border. The Juarez City Market is a popular place to shop. It's run by the city and has an excellent selection of leather goods, blankets, curios, and silver and turquoise jewelry.

Juarez also is home to Mission Guadalupe, the oldest building in the Southwest. It was founded in 1659 and provided food and rest for travelers along the Camino Real. Juarez is home to several museums, including the Museum of History, where the treaties were signed ending the Mexican Revolution.

LORETTO ACADEMY

1300 Hardaway Street
El Paso 79903
(915) 566-8400
www.loretto.org

This private Catholic girls' school in the northeast section of the city includes an illuminated bell tower where someone wearing a nun's habit has been spotted moving about. People who have seen it believe the shadowy figure represents the spirit or energy of one of the late sisters who taught at the school.

The school is named for the Sisters of Loretto, who in 1812 became the first fully American religious congregation with no European ties. The school opened its doors in September 1923, and although the number of sisters who help run the school has declined, Loretto Academy continues to prosper.

McKELLIGON CANYON
1500 McKelligon Canyon Drive
El Paso 79931
(915) 534-0601 or (800) 351-6024

The men's dressing room at this outdoor amphitheater is said to be haunted by the spirit of a construction worker who died while it was being built in 1912. Lights flicker in the dressing room, and the sound of someone running across the room and banging on walls has been reported.

It sounds like the poor guy is trapped inside. But ghosts are known for their ability to move through solid objects, so there must be something more to it than that. Is the banging the sound of a hammer at work? The flickering of lights is reminiscent of the theater lights that go on and off to signal the audience when intermission is coming to an end. Maybe this spirit is playing tricks on the actors.

This 1,500-seat amphitheater in the Franklin Mountains hosts musicals, plays, dances, and performing artists. Performances are held year-round.

THE PLAZA THEATRE
125 Pioneer Plaza
El Paso 79901
(915) 534-0600
http://elpasolive.com/venues/plaza_theatre

This historic downtown theater is said to be haunted by the ghost of a Fort Bliss soldier who died of a heart attack while smoking in the men's room. (See kids: Smoking is bad!) A man dressed in military uniform has been seen near the stairs to the balcony smoking a cigarette despite the fact that smoking is not allowed inside the theater.

The man always disappears before anyone can summon the gumption to approach him and tell him to take that thing outside. Employees have also reported hearing the sound of someone choking in the basement, although no one, as yet, has been able to identify the source.

The Plaza Theatre is one of those old-time theaters that have been refurbished to preserve a portion of the city's history. It's an example of the ornate craftsmanship and design that characterized much of early twentieth-century architecture.

When it opened, this 2,400-seat theater was advertised as the largest of its kind between Dallas and Los Angeles. The architectural style is known as Spanish Colonial Revival. The outside resembles a Spanish mission, while the inside is characterized by intricately painted ceilings, mosaic tile floors, decorative metal railings, and antique furnishings.

Today the theater hosts plays, musicals, choirs, and even rock bands.

SACRED HEART CATHOLIC CHURCH
602 South Oregon Street
El Paso 79901
(915) 532-5447

Sacred Heart Catholic Church is one of the oldest in El Paso. It's located in the oldest part of the city, a mere six blocks from the United States/Mexico border. The ghost who haunts this church is said to be that of a young Mexican woman. The young woman has been spotted in a turn-of-the-twentieth-century bridal gown in the side chapel of Our Lady of Guadalupe. She is seen sitting and weeping over what is believed to be sadness over a marriage that never came to be. Legend has it that the woman died not long after her marriage ceremony fell through, leading one to think that perhaps she died of a broken heart. They say she waits there in hopes that her former lover will return.

SCENIC DRIVE
Rim Road

This 2-mile drive gives you the best view of El Paso, Texas, and Juarez, Mexico. From downtown, take Stanton Street north and make a right on Rim Road. Rim Road will take you all the way around the mountain and through Manhattan Heights, one of El Paso's most attractive historic neighborhoods.

The Rim Road Neighborhood Association has built a sidewalk along a portion of the road to allow visitors to enjoy the scenery by foot. It's a much more relaxing way to take in the view without having to worry about driving.

WOODROW BEAN TRANSMOUNTAIN DRIVE
North El Paso between I-10 and U.S. Highway 54

This mountainous road cuts a path over a section of the Franklin Mountains. Many people traveling this road report seeing a monk and his donkey trudging along. Some say he's protecting a lost gold mine where Spanish missionaries once stored a large fortune.

Historical records indicate that a mine did exist in the area, but so far no one has found it. The road cuts through Franklin Mountains State Park, the largest urban park in the nation at 24,247 acres. Hiking trails can be reached from Transmountain Drive that will eventually provide a 118-mile trail network.

Rock climbing, mountain biking, tent camping, and a limited number of RV parking sites are available.

EL PASO AREA RESTAURANTS
ARDOVINO'S PIZZA
865 North Resler Drive
El Paso 79912
(915) 760-6000
www.ardovinospizza.com

This Ardovino's Pizza restaurant is located in the northern part of the city on your way to the Transmountain Drive. You'll want to stoke up on pizza and other Italian foods before taking a drive across the mountain. If you break down, you might have to rely on the ghost monk and his donkey to give you a lift back to your hotel.

Ardovino's opened in 1961 as a gourmet and Italian food mart. It has expanded through the years to include a pizzeria and delicatessen, and now can be found in three other locations in town: 206 Cincinnati Avenue (central El Paso), 1879 North Zaragoza Drive (east El Paso), and 11100 Sean Haggerty Drive (northeast El Paso). You'll find traditional and gourmet pizzas here, along with house pizzas and sandwiches, salads, and soups.

Joanna's Pizza is made with spinach, tomato, garlic, onion, pesto, feta cheese, and olive oil. It does not come with tomato sauce. The Four Seasons is like four pizzas in one. One quarter is made with sun-dried tomatoes and pesto. Another quarter is topped with artichokes and red peppers, and the third with green chiles and ricotta, and the fourth with spinach and garlic.

For dessert, stick with the traditional Italian dishes of spumoni and cannoli.

BILLY CREWS
1200 Country Club Road
Santa Teresa, NM 88008
(505) 589-2071
www.BillyCrews.net

Located about 200 yards from the state line and well known throughout the El Paso region, Billy Crews serves custom-cut steaks, fresh seafood, prime rib, chicken, lamb, and veal and offers a selection of more than 1,400 wines.

It's open daily for dinner and offers a lunch menu in its lounge. Start your meal with an interesting taste combination with an order of fried green chiles. Those who are more adventurous might want to try an order of "calf fries" (bull testicles).

Custom-cut steaks—T-bone, New York strip, and rib eye— are sold by the pound. You can also order precut steaks, pork chops, veal, and lamb. Or try the Shish-ke-Billy, made with chunks of sirloin, bell peppers, and onions served with seasoned long-grain and wild rice.

For dessert, choose from a selection of homemade pies.

CAFE CENTRAL
109 North Oregon Street
El Paso 79901
(915) 545-2233
www.cafecentral.com

Cafe Central is a downtown El Paso bistro that creates seasonal menus featuring gourmet foods influenced by the region's Southwest palate. It originally opened in 1918 in Juarez and grew into a popular dining and drinking spot for gamblers and cabaret fans.

After Prohibition ended, Cafe Central moved closer to the border and, finally, into downtown El Paso. In 1991 a new owner remade the interior in black and cream and added sprinkles of color via his collection of original art. He restored much of the cafe and added a New Orleans–style courtyard.

Try the yellowtail sashimi as an appetizer, or perhaps the grilled portobello mushroom stuffed with mozzarella and drizzled with a balsamic reduction. Two good entrees are the broiled miso-marinated Chilean sea bass on sweet ginger jasmine rice and the grilled Scottish salmon with clams, mussels, English peas, and heirloom tomatoes in a bright citrus jalapeño broth.

You'll find a great selection of desserts here. You can't go wrong with the chocolate mousse tower with red wine cajeta or the fresh mango colada pie.

The restaurant is located not far from the haunted art museum. Sacred Heart Catholic Church is in the area too.

CATTLE BARON RESTAURANT
1700 Airway Boulevard
El Paso 79922
(915) 779-6633
www.cattlebaron.com

Contrary to popular belief, Texans do eat more than beef. The Cattle Baron proves this in a big way with a huge salad bar along with its famous prime rib, hand-cut steaks, fish, and a relaxing Southwestern atmosphere.

Owner Jeff Wilson opened the first Cattle Baron in 1976 in New Mexico and since then has expanded to several New Mexico and Texas locations. Along with the usual beef offerings, you'll find seafood, chicken, and pork.

Start your meal off with "The Sampler," a combination of green chile wontons, Cajun popcorn shrimp, and cheese sticks. They're served with Thai dipping sauce, tangy marinara, and remoulade. A burger may not sound all that exciting, but the

Cattle Baron makes its burgers with a half a pound of beef charbroiled to your liking. It's then served on a sesame seed bun with your choice of toppings.

Green chile stew is an interesting dish you might want to try. It includes beef sirloin, green chiles, potatoes, onions, tomatoes, and spices served with a homemade flour tortilla. Another mouthwatering entree is the jalapeño rotisserie chicken—half a chicken seasoned with mild jalapeño and lemon and roasted in a rotisserie oven. It's served with onion rings, mashed potatoes, and light gravy.

LA HACIENDA RESTAURANT
1720 West Paisano Drive
El Paso 79922
(915) 533-1919
www.shambala.net/milehigh/lahacienda/index.html

This Mexican restaurant on the banks of the Rio Grande is said to be haunted by the spirit of a woman mourning the loss of her children. She can sometimes be seen walking near the restaurant, weeping and asking for her children, who drowned in the nearby Rio Grande.

The food here is different from the Mexican food found in other parts of the state. Most Mexican food restaurants serve Tex-Mex. The food here is influenced more by pure Mexican cuisine as well as by New Mexico fare, which tends to use more green chiles.

You might start your meal with *flautas de carne deshebradea*—shredded beef rolled in crisp tortillas and served with onion, avocado, sour cream, and salsa. The *caldo de res* can serve as either a large appetizer or a light meal. The recipe for this soup goes back to the 1800s, when Fort Bliss troops often dined on it. It's made with chunky potatoes and beef with tomatoes in a spicy broth.

As an entree, try the tacos de carne asada. It comes with three soft corn tortillas filled with seasoned sirloin tips and served with rice, refried beans, green onions, pico de gallo, and guacamole. Rosa's Roasted Chicken is another winner. It's made with marinated roasted chicken served with two salsas, rice, and charro beans.

EL PASO ORGANIZED TOURS AND PARANORMAL GROUPS

SOUTHWEST PARANORMAL INVESTIGATORS

http://southwestparanormalinvestigations.com/index.html

This group of ghost hunters began in 1992. It investigates "ghosts, poltergeists, UFOs, hauntings, demons, night terrors, legends, religious manifestations"—and anything else that's even remotely spooky.

Membership is free to anyone who is eighteen years of age or older, of stable mind (darn!), and doesn't use alcohol or drugs during investigations. Ghost investigation services are free to those who think they might have a ghost or some other paranormal presence in their home or business. Investigators do accept donations to purchase ghost-hunting equipment and require reimbursement for travel expenses incurred in traveling to and from a haunted site.

One visit to a local house in the mountains resulted in one more-sensitive member of the group feeling "vibes," and two members began to get the feeling (later confirmed by research) that someone had died in the front bedroom. They descended to the darkened basement, sat on the floor in a circle, and lit three candles. One member began to "channel" the spirits, while another heard a loud pop nearby and felt cold chills. One new member became so creeped out that he doubted he would be back. The group finally left the home before midnight, convinced that it possessed a negative aura.

Lubbock

Lubbock, the eleventh-largest city in Texas, is known as the "Hub City" because of its position as the hub of health care, education, and the economy of a multicounty region known as the South Plains. The city itself has a population of nearly 250,000, while the Lubbock metro area is estimated to claim more than 3 million people.

Lubbock is situated in the county of the same name. Thomas Saltus Lubbock, a Confederate colonel and founder of the Texas Rangers (the law enforcement agency, not the baseball team), lent his name to the two entities. The city became the county seat in 1891 and in 1909 was reincorporated as a city.

The city is known for one of the most famous UFO sightings in U.S. history. It occurred in August 1951 when a V-shaped formation of lights appeared over the area. It received national publicity, and a photo taken by a Texas Tech student appeared in *Life* magazine and newspapers nationwide.

Project Blue Book, the U.S. Air Force's official study of the incident, concluded that the UFO was either "night-flying moths" or a formation of plovers (a type of bird). They claimed the underside of the moths or plovers reflected the light from Lubbock's new streetlights. Needless to say, the explanation did not satisfy most people, and the mystery endures.

Texas Tech University is the city's largest employer and home to most if not all of its ghosts. A fraternity house, a ranching heritage center, and several campus buildings are said to be haunted. The ghost of a young boy is believed to haunt the storage room in one campus building, while the wife of a prominent rancher is said to haunt a home at the National Ranching Heritage Center.

LUBBOCK ACCOMMODATIONS

DAYS INN LUBBOCK-TEXAS TECH UNIVERSITY

2401 Fourth Street
Lubbock 79415
(806) 747-7111
www.daysinn.com

The Days Inn will bring you close to the haunted sites found at Texas Tech University. The three-story, ninety-room hotel is across the street from the university and the SBC Jones Stadium, where the popular Texas Tech Red Raiders play football.

This budget hotel offers guests a swimming pool, twenty-four-hour front desk service, free parking, business services, and a free continental breakfast. Rooms come with cable TV, free wireless Internet access, voice mail, hair dryers, and free local calls. Some rooms come with microwaves, refrigerators, and coffeemakers.

STAYBRIDGE SUITES LUBBOCK

2515 Nineteenth Street
Lubbock 79410
(806) 765-8900
www.ihg.com

This Staybridge Suites is just across the street from the haunted Texas Tech University. Take a quick walk onto campus and you'll find yourself face-to-face with a haunted building or two. The three-story hotel offers studio suites with queen-size beds and a larger one-bedroom suite.

Suites come with either a wet bar, microwave, refrigerator, and coffeemaker or a fully equipped kitchen with a two-burner cooktop, microwave, refrigerator, coffeemaker, pots, dishes, and utensils.

Rooms come with free high-speed wireless Internet access, cable TV, modem lines in each room, and a free newspaper. The Staybridge's breakfast buffet comes with eggs, bacon, sausage, fruit, cereals, and coffee. Monday through Thursday, you can relax and enjoy soft drinks and snacks in the lobby. Hotel amenities include a fitness center (last renovated in 2013), laundry/valet service, outdoor pool, hot tub, barbecue area, safe deposit box, and free parking.

WOODROW HOUSE BED & BREAKFAST

2629 Nineteenth Street
Lubbock 79410
(806)793-3330 or (800) 687-5236
www.woodrowhouse.com

The Woodrow House Bed & Breakfast will make ghost hunting in Lubbock convenient and comfortable. Owners David and Dawn Fleming built the three-story, Colonial-style home a few years ago and named it after David's paternal grandfather, George Woodrow Fleming (1914–1972), a rancher, businessman, cotton ginner, grain merchant, and entrepreneur.

Woodrow House has eight guest rooms with private baths. Rooms are decorated in various styles, from Victorian to 1950s to the Texas-themed Lone Star Room. The Santa Fe Caboose in the backyard has been renovated and outfitted with a queen-size bed, private bath, sitting area, and kitchenette.

A full breakfast is served buffet style. The dining room is furnished with an antique sideboard handcrafted in Scotland and a 13-foot-long mahogany dining table that seats as many as sixteen people.

Amenities include a fitness center, a business center, meeting rooms, and dry cleaning. Rooms come with televisions and high-speed wireless Internet access. Common areas include the kitchen and a "gathering room," where guests may watch television, play chess, or assemble a jigsaw puzzle. It's just across the street from the haunted Texas Tech University campus.

LUBBOCK ATTRACTIONS
BETA THETA PI FRATERNITY HOUSE, TEXAS TECH UNIVERSITY
2500 Broadway Boulevard
Lubbock 79409
(806) 742-2011
www.ttu.edu

Texas Tech University may be the most haunted university in Texas. It also seems to be the place where the ghosts in Lubbock like to hang out. All the notable haunted sites in Lubbock can be found on this campus of 24,000 students in the northwest part of town.

Residents of the Beta Theta Pi house have reported several ghost sightings in their home away from home. Pledges report seeing male apparitions watching them through windows, although it's entirely possible that some of the fraternity brothers are behind this.

These pledges also claim that unseen ghosts attend date parties and whisper in the girls' ears that the guy they're dating is gay. Again, this sounds a whole lot like a joke a fraternity brother would play on an unsuspecting pledge. Or maybe the ghosts in Lubbock are homophobic. Who knows?

One pledge reported that a fifth-year senior has been seen at night speaking with shadowy male figures. Are these ghosts? Or is he secretly buying prewritten term papers so he can graduate and avoid becoming a sixth-year senior?

HORN/KNAPP HALL, TEXAS TECH UNIVERSITY
2500 Broadway Boulevard
Lubbock 79409
(806) 742-2011
www.ttu.edu

These two academic buildings are joined together like Siamese twins. The ghost that haunts these buildings has been seen in a third-floor storage room. It's believed to be the spirit of a little boy who died under unknown circumstances.

Late at night, students and faculty members have heard the little boy throwing a ball down the stairs and laughing. Knock on the door to the storage room, and sometimes he'll knock back. I dare you to open the door!

NATIONAL RANCHING HERITAGE CENTER, TEXAS TECH UNIVERSITY
2500 Broadway Boulevard
Lubbock 79409
(806) 742-0498 or (806) 742-0500
www.ttu.edu

The ghost that haunts this center is believed to be the wife of the rancher who built the original two-story white house on this fourteen-acre site.

Police have responded several times to calls about a woman standing in one of the upper windows after hours. They've responded so many times, in fact, that they no longer take the calls seriously. Not that they don't respond. Let's just say they give these calls a low priority. The reason? The woman always vanishes by the time they arrive.

Thirty restored structures here show ranching's evolution from the early trail drivers' days of the one-room cabin to that of a wealthy rancher in a turn-of-the-twentieth-century Victorian home. Other structures include a bunkhouse, blacksmith shop, corrals, windmills, chuck wagons, and a coal-burning locomotive.

THOMPSON HALL, TEXAS TECH UNIVERSITY
2500 Broadway Boulevard
Lubbock 79409
(806) 742-2011
www.ttu.edu

Medical students used to take gross anatomy in this building before the university erected a separate building for the medical school. The word *gross* isn't used in this instance to describe what the medical students saw, and there may not be any truth to the rumor that the building once served as a morgue.

There are reports, however, of people being spotted moving around inside the building when no one is supposed to be there. That might not be so bad were it not for the fact that these floors are restricted from public access. Not only that, you need a key to get onto these floors, and access is electronically monitored.

Yet there are no records to indicate that anyone unlocked a door to get on those particular floors. Ghosts, it seems, don't need keys. The lights in this building go on and off for no apparent reason, and sometimes, when a person stands directly beneath a light, the light will turn on, as if the ghosts want to take a better look.

LUBBOCK RESTAURANTS

COWAMONGUS

Indiana Avenue at Main Avenue
Lubbock 79409
(806) 742-2882
www.depts.ttu.edu/cowamongus/westerncow/Home.htm

This is quite possibly the most unusual place for a successful restaurant. It's located on the first floor of the Animal and Food Sciences Building on the campus of Texas Tech University.
There's no sign and no parking. You'll find it just off the main lobby.
The words *animal*, *science*, and *delicious* don't often go together. But in the case of Cowamongus (get it?), the three words go together like *steak* and *potatoes*. This small restaurant is also a retail store for the Texas Tech Meat Lab.
Again, that doesn't sound all that delectable until you consider the fact that, hey, at least the meat is fresh. The restaurant itself isn't haunted, but since it's so close to campus (five blocks), you'll be close to all the paranormal action.
The menu here is limited but good. Try the prime rib sandwich or one of the fresh wraps offered. You can get made-to-order breakfast tacos, along with salads, soups, and homemade custards.

LA DIOSA CELLARS

901 Seventh Street
Lubbock 79401
(806) 744-3600
www.ladiosacellars.com

La Diosa Cellars is a combination restaurant, winery, and coffee shop set amid a Bohemian-style tavern in Lubbock's Depot

District. This colorful and comfortable restaurant is a great place for wine by the glass, an Italian coffee, and tapas.

The only winery operating inside the Lubbock city limits, La Diosa (Spanish for "the Goddess") produces 2,000 cases of wine each year. Varietals include cabernet sauvignon, merlot, Syrah, Sangiovese, Viognier, and sangria. Several house blends include Bella Rosa, Bella Riojo, and Bella Blanca. La Diosa also serves wines from other West Texas wineries as well as select Hill Country wineries.

As for food, you can choose from wraps, grilled sandwiches, tapas, and desserts. The Josephine, a spicy West Texas wrap, looks good. It's made with a tomato basil tortilla with roasted chicken, grilled peppers and onions, and jack cheese served with black beans and pico de gallo. Another good choice is the España grilled sandwich, made with baked ham, Anaheim chiles, jack cheese, and chipotle aioli.

You'll find a creative variety of tapas here. A couple of good ones are the Rebecca (hot French brie topped with red jalapeño preserves and toasted almonds served with crostinis) and Besitos (baked jalapeño halves stuffed with shrimp, jack cheese, and bacon).

For dessert, try the Sinful Chocolate Truffle Cake or the amazing Awesome Carrot Cake.

WEST TEXAS DAY TRIPS
AND GETAWAY WEEKENDS

Feel like taking a drive? A loooooong drive? Then fill your tank and empty your bladder. It's time for a trip to the remote reaches of West Texas to visit two historic forts haunted by soldiers who were once stationed there. If you're lucky, you can also experience one of the world's most mysterious events known as "the Marfa Lights."

I've broken this up into two trips—one leaving from **El Paso** and the other from **Lubbock.**

The first trip leaves southeast from El Paso along I-10 to Van Horn. From there, take U.S. Highway 90 southeast. Just south of Valentine, take Highway 505 and then Texas Highway 166 East. Turn left on Texas Highway 17 and follow it to **Fort Davis National Historic Site** (432-426-3224, ext. 20). The drive will take about four hours.

Fort Davis is maintained by the federal parks system and is considered an excellent example of an Indian Wars frontier military post in the Southwest. From 1854 to 1891, Fort Davis protected settlers, mail coaches, and freight wagons traveling along the Trans-Pecos portion of the San Antonio–El Paso Road.

As you might expect, the ghosts of several soldiers who served at the fort are believed to haunt this place. The walls of the former post hospital are said to change colors, and a presence has been felt inside. The hospital is being restored. Apparitions of soldiers have been reported in other parts of the fort along with unexplained cold spots.

The ghost of a young woman supposedly abducted by Indians is also said to haunt the fort. An Alabama woman named Alice Walpole disappeared from the fort during a Confederate troop occupation, according to Lisa Farwell's *Haunted Texas Vacations*. Legend has it she was picking white roses along a nearby creek when she went missing.

Her ghost showed up not long after that, and it is said she haunts the old fort to this day. Farwell writes that the scent of roses precedes her appearance, and white roses sometimes are found around the fort even when they're out of season.

The fort consists mostly of former barracks that sit in a row at the foot of the Davis Mountains. Expect to spend around two hours touring the fort, hiking to nearby Davis Mountain State Park, and enjoying the occasional living-history programs, including artillery demonstrations.

For a great view and a get-away-from-it-all feeling, stay at the **Indian Lodge in Davis Mountains State Park** (432-426-3254, http://tpwd.texas.gov/state-parks/indian-lodge). The lodge has thirty-nine units, one hundred camping sites, and a restaurant. The **Veranda Inn** (210 Court Avenue, 888-383-2847, www.theveranda.com) is a good choice for those who want to stay in the town of Fort Davis. This highly acclaimed historic inn and guesthouse is enclosed inside walled gardens and features attractive courtyards. Rooms and suites come with private baths. Breakfast is served each morning.

Blue Mountain Bistro (432-426-3244, www.hotellimpia .com/restaurant) in the **Hotel Limpia** in Fort Davis is open for dinner seven days a week and offers a breakfast buffet on weekends. Tapas, country French cooking, and char-grilled Texas rib-eye steaks are among its specialties. **Stone Village Market** (507 North State Street, 432-426-2226), also in Fort Davis, is open daily from 7:00 a.m. to 7:00 p.m. It's an unassuming store where you can stock up on Big Bend coffee beans, grab some groceries, and order a breakfast taco made with locally sourced ingredients. Several made-while-you-wait sandwiches are on the menu here, along with soups, salads, and fresh-baked cookies and muffins.

As long as you're out this way, you might as well take a drive south to Marfa and search for the **Marfa Lights.** This small town of 2,100 people 20 miles south of Fort Davis attracts visitors from all over the world, who travel to a viewing area 10 miles east of town to see a mysterious phenomenon. The Marfa Lights bounce around in the sky, vanish, and reappear on clear nights.

So far, no one has been able to explain them. Some say they are caused by swamp gas, radioactive bursts, or ball lightning. Some attribute them to headlights and taillights of cars in the mountains. Still others claim they're caused by space aliens or ghosts. These lights appear only ten to twelve times a year, so, if you see them, count yourself among the fortunate.

The second day trip or weekend getaway will take you from Lubbock to San Angelo. **San Angelo,** a city of almost 100,000, is located on the eastern edge of West Texas, if that makes any sense. It's home to **San Angelo State University** and **Fort Concho** (630 South Oakes Street, 325-481-2646), both of which are said to be haunted.

To get there from Lubbock, take U.S. Highway 84 southeast until you get there. The distance is around 190 miles, and it will take around four hours to make the journey. The site most commonly mentioned when discussing San Angelo ghosts is Fort Concho, built in 1867 to protect frontier settlements. Fort Concho is a National Historic Landmark and includes twenty-three original and restored structures.

Numerous ghosts are said to haunt this place. Many of the soldiers who were stationed here, including some buffalo soldiers, are said to haunt the old fort. Officers Quarters No. 1 is said to be haunted by a little girl who died of an unknown illness in the upstairs section. Occasional apparitions of soldiers have been reported, and cold spots give visitors the chills from time to time.

The **Housing Office at San Angelo State University** is believed to be haunted by the ghost of a young woman murdered there in the 1970s by an ROTC cadet. The would-be soldier is said to have flown into a violent rage when his amorous advances were rejected. Little is known about the woman or the way she haunts this building. An unidentified young woman has been spotted from time to time, and cold spots have been reported.

Santa Rita Park, located at the corner of South Madison and South Jefferson Streets, is alleged to be the home of a ghost named Marie, who reportedly once resided in the area and enjoyed taking walks in the park. Some believe Marie plays with stray dogs at night. They can be seen jumping around playfully and barking excitedly as though they are playing with someone.

Marie is said to sit on a bench near an elementary school that faces the park. People who have been there say that if you sit on the bench, you'll feel a chill and a sense of restlessness.

For a place to stay while in San Angelo, try the **The Clarion Hotel** (441 Rio Concho Drive, 325-658-2828, www.choicehotels .com/texas/san-angelo/clarion-hotels/txa45). This downtown hotel isn't far from Fort Concho or Santa Rita Park. The 148-room hotel is across the street from the San Angelo Convention Center. When you get hungry, try **Miss Hattie's Restaurant and Cathouse Lounge** (26 East Concho Avenue, 325-653-0570, www.misshattiesrestaurant.com) for American-style food, **Chadbourne Street Deli** (109 South Chadbourne Street, 325-658-6480), or **Zentner's Daughter Steak House** (1901 Knickerbocker Road, 325-949-2821, www.zentnersdaughter.com).

An alternative to San Angelo is a 90-minute drive north to **Amarillo.** Amarillo is home to several haunted houses that open in October for Halloween, including the **6th Street Massacre** (3015 SW 6th Avenue, 806-337-0749, http://center citymayhem.com/HauntAbout.html). This attraction is the creation of the masterminds behind the former City Center Massacre (voted Amarillo's scariest haunt in 2005), West Campus Massacre, and 7th Street Massacre.

The 6th Street Massacre experience is based on the legend of the McKill family, who are said to have fled from Tennessee to the Texas panhandle. This dysfunctional family supposedly kidnapped people in the 1930s as they traveled through the area to escape the Oklahoma "Dust Bowl."

Locals found out what the McKills were doing and decided they weren't good for the city's image. So they burned their house down and may have even canceled their chamber of commerce membership. The McKills escaped into the woods and haven't been heard from since . . . until now . . . at Halloween. While you're in Amarillo, for a uniquely Texas experience visit the **Big Texan Steak Ranch** (7701 I-40 East, 800-657-7177, www.bigtexan.com). If you can eat their renowned 72-ounce steak dinner in an hour or less, you eat for free. In the mood for a steak of the chicken-fried variety? Then try **Country Pride Restaurant** (5909 Wineinger Road, 806-373-3592). For several years running, their chicken-fried steak has been voted the best around, and the enchiladas are highly recommended too.

SUGGESTED READING AND WEBSITES

PRINT

A Texas Guide to Restaurants, Taverns, and Inns. Robert Wlodarski and Anne Powell Wlodarski. Republic of Texas, 2001.

Best Tales of Texas Ghosts. Docia Schultz Williams and Reneta Byrne. Republic of Texas, 1998.

Ghosts in the Graveyard: Texas Cemetery Tales. Olyve Abbott. Republic of Texas, 2001.

Ghosts of Denton: The History of the Mysteries in a Small Texas Town. Shelly Tucker. 2014.

The Ghosts of Fort Brown: An Informal Study of Brownsville Folklore and Parapsychology. The Arnulfo L. Oliveira Literary Society, 2003.

Ghost Stories of Texas. Ed Syers. Texian Press, 1981.

Ghost Tales of Texas. Jo Anne Christensen. Lone Pine Publishing, 2001.

Haunted Texas Vacations: The Complete Ghostly Guide. Lisa Farwell. Westcliffe Publishers, 2000.

I'll Tell You a Tale—An Anthology. Frank J. Dobie. University of Texas Press, 1984.

WEBSITES

Corpus Christi Spook Central Group
www.ccspookcentral.com

Dagulf's Ghost
http://dagulf0.tripod.com

Ghost Hunters of Texas
www.ghosthuntersoftexas.com

Ghost Hunting 101
http://ghosthunting101.com

Ghost Tour Directory—Texas
www.ghosttourdirectory.com/ghost-tours/united-states/texas-tx/

The Ghosts of Fort Brown
http://blue.utb.edu/ghostsoffortbrown/

Hollow Hill
http://encounterghosts.com/hollow-hill-articles-are-here-now/

Lone Star Spirits
www.lsspi.org

Paranormal Investigations of North Texas
www.shadowlands.net

Paranormal Investigators of Texas
www.paratexas.com

Southwest Ghost Hunters Association
www.sgha.net

TexasEscapes.com
www.texasescapes.com

Texas Paranormal Investigators
http://txghosthunters.com/

Unexplainable.net
www.unexplainable.net

West Texas Paranormal Society
www.westtexasparanormal.org

SPOOKTACULAR PLACES TO SPEND HALLOWEEN

Most kids in Texas still celebrate Halloween the old-fashioned way. They go trick-or-treating door to door in their neighborhoods or, in some cases, travel to other neighborhoods known for giving out good candy.

A number of alternative sites have sprung up in recent years in malls, community centers, and schools. Children at these events enjoy candy, food, games, and maybe a scary story or two. Some parents just feel safer taking their kids to something like this.

It seems as if every year a new haunted house opens up with the sole purpose of scaring the heck out of paying customers. While some operate on Halloween only, others gleefully scare people on Halloween and every weekend in October. Some exist to raise funds for charity, while others are purely capitalistic ventures (the horror!).

Following are nine top "spooktacular" places in Texas to spend Halloween:

1. 6th Street Massacre (Amarillo)

3015 SW 6th Avenue, (806) 337-0749, http://centercitymayhem.com/HauntAbout.html. *See page 256.*

Formerly known as the Center City Massacre, this attraction has been voted Amarillo's scariest haunt. This haunted house is based on the legend of the McKill family (what a coincidence that their name would have the word *kill* in it!).

The McKills are said to have kidnapped and murdered people in the 1930s as they traveled through the area to escape the infamous "Dust Bowl" of Oklahoma. Locals discovered what they were up to and torched their house. Several McKills escaped into the woods and were never heard from again.

2. Cutting Edge Haunted House (Fort Worth)
1701 East Lancaster Avenue (intersection of I-30 and U.S. Highway 287), (817) 348-8444, www.cuttingedgehaunted house.com. *See page 197.*

The Cutting Edge claims to be the largest haunted house ever—a claim backed by the Guinness World Record organization, which declared it to be "The Longest Haunted House in the World" in 2009. It's located in a 235,000-square-foot warehouse in downtown Fort Worth. It's also been featured on the Travel Channel and was voted by many haunted house-rating organizations (including HauntedHouses.com, America Haunts, and Fangoria) for several years as one of the top haunted houses in the country.

Built in the 1920s, this warehouse is home each Halloween—and other October nights—to Texas Chainsaw Massacre ghosts, gothic horrors, frightful haunted mansion props, raging phantoms, and screams that will have you shaking in your cowboy boots.

3. Dungeon of Doom (Arlington)
201 West Main Street, (817) 275-4600, www.dungeonofdoom texas.com. *See page 206.*

The Dungeon of Doom is a permanent fixture in the basement of the Arlington Museum of Art. Proceeds go to support children's art education programs. An ensemble of dedicated actors use headphones to cue each other and perform "bits" designed to scare the bejeezus out of you.

Dungeon of Doom was voted "Best Haunted House" three times by the *Dallas Observer* newspaper and received "5 Bloody Daggers" from the *Fort Worth Star-Telegram.*

4. Fearesta (San Antonio)

201 East Grayson Avenue, (210) 299-1555, www.fearesta.com. *See page 60.*

With as many ghosts as San Antonio has, it's no surprise that locals celebrate Halloween here with haunted houses and parties. Fearesta (formerly Nightmare on Grayson) is a fun-spirited festival that celebrates the scary while providing enough family entertainment to make it kid-friendly too.

This festival is in an older San Antonio neighborhood and features a fun "festevil" that includes food, beverages, and entertainers—flame throwers, magicians, face painters, tarot card readers, and palm readers.

5. Port Isabel Day of the Dead Celebration

317 East Railroad Avenue, (956) 943-7602, www.portisabelmu seums.com/dod. *See page 120.*

Dia de los Muertos, or Day of the Dead, is celebrated at the end of October in many South Texas towns. This Mexican tradition pays tribute to those who have passed on to the next world. Although it may sound a tad morbid, Day of the Dead is anything but.

In Port Isabel, the day is commemorated with various programs by the Museums of Port Isabel. They include exhibits of Day of the Dead altars created by local college students, cemetery tours, lectures, music, dances, poems, and stories—all with a deadly theme. You can learn how to make your own Day of the Dead altars as well as skull-shaped candy.

When darkness falls, enjoy a scary movie projected on the side of the Port Isabel Lighthouse.

6. ScreamWorld (Houston)

2225 North Sam Houston Parkway West, www.screamworld .com. *See page 15.*

Voted Houston's scariest haunted attraction by the *Houston Chronicle* and Houstonhaunts.com, ScreamWorld consists of five scary attractions in one location: The Swamp, "considered the most high-tech haunted attraction in Houston"; the Edge of Darkness, a good ol' haunted house; Jake's Slaughterhouse (as if a traditional meat packing plant isn't bloody enough); Zombie Graveyard, capitalizing on the latest horror craze; and the Clown Asylum Maze, a maze so intricate that its creators claim it could drive you insane.

7. Terror on the Bayou (Jefferson)
1602 Highway 49 East, (903) 665-6464, www.terroronthe bayou.com. *See page 211.*

Jefferson, one of the most haunted towns in Texas, is also home to Terror on the Bayou, a compilation of three frightening attractions in one site. The Creepy Screamin' Maze, the Runaway Fright Train, and the Haunted Forest Walk will scare and entertain you.

The Creepy Screamin' Maze is a post-apocalyptic wasteland set in a corn maze. Not only do you have to find your way out, but you also have to survive assaults from the horrific-looking survivors of Armageddon.

The Runaway Fright Train is a 5-mile-long "haunted house" on wheels that travels along the tracks of the Jefferson & Cypress Bayou Railway. G-rated rides last 45 minutes, while PG-13 treks last an hour. PG-13 rides are more frightening than the G-rated rides, which are suitable for children.

The Haunted Forest Walk is a trek through the "bottoms" of Cypress Bayou. It includes the 100-foot-long Tunnel of Doom. Along the way, you'll encounter all sorts of scary creatures hell-bent on making you scream.

8. Thrillvania (Terrell)

I-20 and Wilson Road, (972) 524-2868, www.thrillvania.com.
See page 173.

This nationally acclaimed attraction east of Dallas features haunted attractions, a midway, food, beverages, and a haunted store. Some of the attractions include:

- *Haunted Verdun Manor*, the former home of Baron Michael Verdun and his wife, Lady Cassandra, who together hosted fiendish masquerades around the turn of the twentieth century. It is said the baron, his wife, and the fiendish human/animal hybrids they created haunt the rotted mansion and overgrown cemetery.
- *Cassandra's Labyrinth of Terror*, a twisted journey through the equally twisted memories of Lady Cassandra D'Arque, who, along with her husband, was killed and decapitated by an angry mob (as opposed to a friendly mob). The labyrinth is filled with vignettes from her disturbing past.
- *Dr. Lycan's Trail of Torment*, where this onetime psychologist tries to regain his sanity by luring naive and curious humans each October. The good doctor, who once assisted the Baron Verdun in his dastardly experiments, has tried to create a virtual guide into his psyche. Be careful! The doc has released his human/monster creations. You never know when you might bump into one.
- *Granny Lupus's Séance Theatre* allows you to witness physical manifestations of the spirits that haunt the Verdun estate. Ectoplasmic entities and fearless flying phantoms make this séance one you will never forget.

SPECIAL INDEXES

MOST MACABRE MUSEUMS

Austin
Neill-Cochran House Museum, 135

Edinburg
Museum of South Texas History, 115

El Paso
El Paso Museum of Art, 234

Fort Worth
Log Cabin Village, 199

Galveston
Ashton Villa House Museum, 31

Houston
Civil War Museum, 9
Griffin Memorial House/Tomball Museum Center, 11
Spring Historical Museum, 16

San Antonio
McNay Art Museum, 61
Witte Museum, 65

TWITCHIEST TOURS

Alamo Ghost Tours, 73
Austin Ghost Tours, 144
Fort Worth Stockyards Ghost Tour, 205
Ghost Tours of Galveston, 38
Hauntings History of San Antonio Ghost Hunt, 71
The Walking Ghost Tours of Old Town Spring, 26

EERIEST EATS

Austin
The Tavern, 142

Corpus Christi
Black Beard's on the Beach, 80

Dallas
Snuffer's Bar and Grill, 176

Galveston
Mediterranean Chef, 36

Houston
La Carafe Wine Bar, 19
Puffabelly's Old Depot Restaurant, 20
Treebeards, 23
Wunsche Bros. Cafe and Saloon, 24

San Antonio
The Church Bistro and Theatre at King William, 68
Schilo's Delicatessen, 70

SCARIEST STAYS

Austin
Austin's Inn at Pearl Street, 123
Carrington's Bluff Bed & Breakfast, 124
The Driskill Hotel, 126

Dallas
Hotel Adolphus, 161
La Quinta Inn & Suites Dallas Downtown, 163

Fort Worth
Miss Molly's Bed and Breakfast Hotel, 193
The Texas White House, 195

New Braunfels
Faust Hotel & Brewing Co., 146
Prince Solms Inn Bed & Breakfast, 147

San Antonio
Emily Morgan Hotel, 51
Menger Hotel, 54
Sheraton Gunter Hotel, 56
The St. Anthony—A Wyndham Historic Hotel, 57

ABOUT THE AUTHORS

Scott Williams is the coauthor of *The Insiders' Guide to Corpus Christi*. He is a full-time freelance writer who has spent the past three decades as a reporter and writer for newspapers, magazines, websites, and book publishers. He lives in Corpus Christi, Texas.

Donna Ingham is a Texas author and storyteller who lives in Spicewood, just west of Austin. She has written five other books about the Lone Star State and continues to collect tales both true and tall. Her website is donnaingham.com.